JN084382

Broadcast: ABC WORLD NEWS TONIGHT

2

Shigeru Yamane
Kathleen Yamane

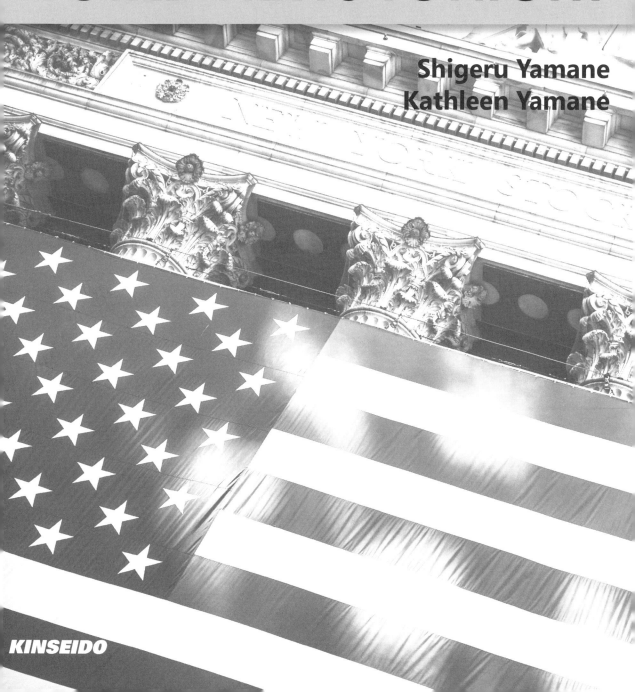

KINSEIDO

Kinseido Publishing Co., Ltd.
3-21 Kanda Jimbo-cho, Chiyoda-ku,
Tokyo 101-0051, Japan

First published 2020 by Kinseido Publishing Co., Ltd.

Foreword

World News Tonight, the flagship news program of the American Broadcast Company, is enjoyed by millions of Americans each evening at 6:30. With its reputation for balanced, fair reporting by a news team who take a personalized look at what's happening around the world and report it with heart, the show is consistently at the top of the evening news ratings.

Since the publication of this textbook series began more than three decades ago, the popular newscasts have become part of the learning experience of thousands of Japanese students, as well. This text is the second in our new series, incorporating several changes that we feel will enhance the learning experience. As always, we have made every effort to select stories that are not only important but will also make young adults think a little bit harder about the world outside of Japan. This book includes a stimulating cross section of topics from the Virgin Galactic space flight and the Special Olympics to the American college admissions scandal. Students will learn about Prime Minister Abe and President Trump's "sumo diplomacy" as well as enjoying astounding new visuals from Antarctica. The stories will take you all across the U.S. and beyond, introducing you to ISIS brides, the first responders at Notre Dame Cathedral and retired U.S. military returning to Vietnam and reconnecting with their former enemies. We feel certain that you will find them all to be as fascinating as we do.

Back in 1987, no one associated with this ABC World News textbook project imagined that the series would have such longevity and touch the lives of so many students. We believe that adopting authentic broadcast news materials for classroom use is a powerful way to build English skills while also helping students to become more knowledgeable about world affairs and to develop the critical thinking skills necessary for all young people in today's increasingly interconnected world. Many of our students also tell us that using the text was good preparation for the TOEFL and TOEIC exams and for job interviews. To the students using *Broadcast: ABC WORLD NEWS TONIGHT 2*, remember that the skills that you develop using this book can be applied to other news shows, even when the course is over.

We sincerely hope that you will challenge yourselves to become more aware of world events and be inspired to follow the news more closely. Happy studying!

January 2020

Shigeru Yamane
Kathleen Yamane

まえがき

近年，日常生活において情報源としてインターネットの活用がますます盛んになってきている。このような高度な情報化社会では，不正確な情報や見方の偏った情報も多くあふれている。学生諸君は，何が本当に自分に役立つ正しい情報か，情報の「質」を見極める能力を身につける必要があるのではないだろうか。

一般的に，テレビニュースからの情報は信頼性が高いといわれている。本書はアメリカの3大ネットワーク（ABC，CBS，NBC）の一つである，ABC放送からのテレビニュース番組を録画し，それを文字化した上で，テキスト用に編集したものである。収録したニュースは米国東部標準時間夕方6時30分から毎日放送されているABC放送の看板ニュース番組*ABC World News Tonight*である。

1948年に始まり，長い歴史を誇るこのABC放送のニュース番組は，ピーター・ジェニングズなど，多くの人気キャスターを生み出してきた。2014年にディビッド・ミュアがアンカーパーソンに抜擢され，さらに人気が高まった。2015年3月には「アメリカで最も多く視聴されている夕方のニュース番組」となり，アメリカ国内でも絶大な人気を保ちながら，質の高い情報を毎日提供し続けている。

今回も，そのABC放送の看板番組の中から，大学生が学ぶにふさわしい多種多様なニュースを15本厳選し，収録することができた。アメリカ国内のニュースだけではなく，ニュージーランドにおける銃規制やノートルダム寺院火災など，世界のニュースも含まれている。さらに，アメリカの移民政策，名門大学で裏口入学の事件など，本書で取り上げた現在社会が抱えるさまざまなトピックを学ぶことを通じて，学生諸君にはニュースの理解を深めながら，自分の意見も持ってもらいたい。また，身近で親しみやすい話題としては，小学校で活躍するシニアたちの話，考えさせる話題としては，病と闘う３歳児の治療方法をめぐるニュースなども多く収録した。

ニュースを収録した映像は、専用のウェブサイトplus+Media上でストリーミング視聴することができる。ぜひ，学生諸君にはこの映像を繰り返し見てもらいたい。アメリカの家庭で毎日アメリカ人が見ている良質のニュース番組に触れ，信頼できる情報をもとに英語を学んでもらいたい。

本書は1987年に*TV News from the U.S.A.*として始まった。その後，1999年から*ABC World News*として20年間毎年出版され続けた。また2019年には，さまざまな箇所に改良を加え，*Broadcast: ABC WORLD NEWS TONIGHT*と書名を変更し生まれ変わった。アメリカABC放送のニュースを利用した本シリーズは，今回で通算27冊目になり、お陰様で毎回たいへん好評を頂いている。2010年度には外国語教育メディア学会（LET）から，本教材の開発に対して，LET学会賞の「教材開発賞」を受賞する栄誉を頂いた。今後もさらにより良い教材開発の努力を続けていきたい。

最後になったが，テキスト作成に際して毎回大変お世話になっている金星堂のみなさん，今回もこころよく版権を許可してくださったアメリカABC放送に心から感謝の意を表したい。

2020年1月

山根　繁

Kathleen Yamane

Broadcast: ABC WORLD NEWS TONIGHT

2

Table of Contents

News Story 1
Legacy of Captain Mariner 1
女性の道を切り開いた海軍パイロット

News Story 2
America Strong: Foster Grandparents 7
小学校で活躍するシニアたち

News Story 3
Assault Weapons Ban in New Zealand 12
ニュージーランド, 銃規制へ

News Story 4
Sumo Diplomacy 19
トランプ大統領をおもてなし

News Story 5
American ISIS Bride 27
帰国を望むイスラム国の花嫁たち

News Story 6
Milestone Mission: Virgin Galactic 33
宇宙旅行時代に向けて

News Story 7
Notre Dame Cathedral: Full Damage Revealed 38
ノートルダム寺院の現状

News Story 8
Three-year-old Boy Fighting Cancer 44
病と闘う3歳児の治療方法をめぐって

News Story 9
Journey to the Edge 49
クジラの生態から見る地球環境

News Story 10
Special Olympics Funding Furor 55
特別オリンピック予算カットか?

News Story 11
American Heroes in Vietnam 61
ベトナム戦争の英雄たちが再会

News Story 12
Measles Outbreak Quarantine in L.A. 67
はしか感染, 全米で広がる

News Story 13
Mayors Challenge Trump 74
市長たち, 政府の移民政策に立ち向かう

News Story 14
Columbine: 20 Years Later 81
コロンバイン事件を悼む人々

News Story 15
College Scandal Shock Waves 88
名門大学で裏口入学

Appendix
   Map of the United States
   TVニュース英語とは
   最近のTVニュースに現れた略語

Legacy of Captain Mariner

Before You Watch the News

Air Date: February 2, 2019
Duration: 2′ 02″

Preview Questions

1. Who was Captain Mariner?
——マリナー大佐はどのような人物でしたか。

2. What were some of her firsts?
——彼女が初めて成し遂げたことは何でしたか。

Warm-up Exercises

A Vocabulary Check: Choose the correct definition for each of the words below.

1. soar (   )   **a.** obstacle; hurdle

2. tactical (   )   **b.** battle; fight

3. barrier (   )   **c.** strategic

4. combat (   )   **d.** to chart or record

5. log (   )   **e.** to fly; to rise up into the sky

B Fill in the blanks with appropriate expressions from the Vocabulary Check above. Change the word form where necessary.

1. My uncle was in the Army, but he was never involved in active (   ).

2. Even though the home team had a (   ) advantage, we beat them by five goals!

3. We watched the eagle (   ) through the sky.

4. If we keep going at this pace, we may be able to (   ) six kilometers today.

5. It's getting a bit easier for foreigners to find work here, but there are still (   ).

News Story [2′ 02″]

T. Llamas: Finally tonight, we celebrate a hero on her final mission. She wanted to fly before she could even drive and soared right into history. She's America Strong.

Over the skies of eastern Tennessee, a first, the missing man formation flown entirely **1.** _____ _____. All in honor of Navy pilot Rosemary Mariner, call sign Viper, the first woman to fly a tactical fighter jet.

Commander S. Uttecht, U.S. Navy fighter pilot: It's really awesome to be part of, uh, an all-female crew. Something that the Navy has never done.

T. Llamas: Mariner died January 24th, at the age of 65, after fighting cancer for five years. Throughout her career she fought to break barriers and **2.** _____. In 1973, she was one of eight women to get her wings from the Navy. The next year she became a fighter pilot. It was just the first of her many firsts — the first woman to land on aircraft carriers, she flew in Desert Storm, and was the first woman to command a squadron.

She was a shining beacon for the female pilots who followed in her footsteps, including those flying over her funeral today.

Lieutenant Commander P. Blok, U.S. Navy fighter pilot: **3.** _____

5

whether I could fly combat roles in today's Navy, and more doors are opening every day.

T. Llamas: Mariner always wanted to fly. Her father, an Air Force pilot, died in a plane crash when she was just three, but that didn't stop her. She washed planes **4.** _____, later enlisting, serving her country while also piloting women's rights in the military.

10

Mariner retired as a captain in 1997. She logged 3,500 military flight hours, but her impact in the skies and on the ground — immeasurable.

15

T. Mariner, husband: **5.** _____, but to be the first person that opened the door, but left it open for others to follow her through.

T. Llamas: So tonight, we honor the legacy of Captain Mariner. Thank you for watching. I'm Tom Llamas in New York. *GMA* and *This Week* in the morning, and I'll see you right back here tomorrow night. Have a great evening. Good night.

20

Notes **America Strong**「アメリカ・ストロング〈*ABC World News Tonight* には America Strong（強くあれ，アメリカ）というアメリカを元気にしてくれるニュースを紹介するコーナーがある〉」 **missing man formation**「ミッシング・マン・フォーメーション〈殉職者や生前に功績のあった人への追悼飛行で組まれる編隊。飛行中，編隊の中の1機が離脱して急上昇し，その人が天に昇るさまを演じるのが特徴。今回は，missing woman formation〉」 **in honor of ~**「～に哀悼の意を表して；～のめい福を祈って」 **call sign**「コールサイン〈アメリカ海軍の戦闘機パイロットが，友軍機との交信時に互いに使う呼び名〉」 **tactical fighter jet**「戦術戦闘機」 **Commander**「大佐」 **get her wings from ~**「～に入隊した（パイロットの資格を得た）〈もともと get one's wings は，仕事の経験を積むという意味〉」 **Desert Storm**「砂漠の嵐作戦（Operation Desert Storm）〈1991 年からの湾岸戦争「砂漠の嵐作戦」に参戦した〉」 **command a squadron**「(海軍) 飛行隊を指揮した」 **shining beacon**「輝ける先導者〈ビーコンは，点滅する光で飛行機を導く灯台，航路標識のこと。マリナーさんのお陰で女性パイロットの道が開けた〉」 **followed in her footsteps**「彼女の足跡をたどった；彼女の先例に倣った；彼女の歩んだ道を歩んだ」 **flying over her funeral**「彼女の葬儀（が行われていた）上空を追悼飛行

した」 **Lieutenant Commander**「少佐」 **fly combat roles**「コンバットロールに就く（戦闘機の
パイロットなどがつく実戦を想定した任務）」 **enlisting**「入隊した」 **piloting ~**「〜を導いた；〜の
先駆者になった」 **captain**「大佐」 **follow her through**「（彼女が最初に開けた扉から，その後もず
っと）後に続く」 **legacy**「遺産；レガシー」 ***GMA***「『グッドモーニング・アメリカ』(*Good
Morning America*)〈ABC 放送によるモーニングショー〉」 ***This Week***「『ジス・ウィーク』〈ABC 放
送の政治討論番組で日曜の朝に放送される〉」

After — You Watch the News

Exercises

A Listen to the CD and fill in the blanks in the text. ◉ CD 02

B Mark the following sentences true (T) or false (F) according to the information in the news story.

(　　) **1.** Mariner learned to fly before she learned to drive a car.

(　　) **2.** Capt. Mariner was honored by an all-female crew at her funeral.

(　　) **3.** Mariner became interested in flying from washing planes with her father.

(　　) **4.** She became the U.S. Navy's first female fighter pilot in 1973.

(　　) **5.** According to her husband, Mariner accomplished many firsts in order to become famous.

(　　) **6.** Mariner retired from the Navy 24 years after getting her wings.

C Translate the following Japanese into English. Then listen to the CD and practice the conversation with your partner. ◉ CD 03

A: Look at those birds soaring in perfect formation.

B: Those aren't birds! **1.** _____.

A: Fighter pilots? There's no war going on.

B: Haven't you heard? Today is Rosemary Mariner's funeral. An all-female crew is honoring her legacy.

A: Of course. **2.** Because of her, _____
_____, right?

B: That's right. **3.** Actually, _____
_____.

A: Wow! That would be awesome. We women can do anything nowadays.

1. ミッシング・マン・フォーメーションを組んでいる戦闘機のパイロットたちですよ。

2. 彼女のお陰で，ますます多くの女性が戦闘機のパイロットになっていますね。

3. 実は，卒業後は海軍に入隊しようと思っています。

D Summary Practice: Fill in the blanks with suitable words beginning with the letters indicated.

◎ CD 04

Captain Rosemary Mariner, the first female (¹· **f**   ) (²· **p**   )
in the U.S. Navy, lost her five-year battle with (³· **c**   ) on January
24th. To honor her (⁴· **l**   ), her funeral included a
(⁵· **m**   ) (⁶· **m**   ) formation flown exclusively by
(⁷· **f**   ) fighter pilots. The daughter of a pilot, Mariner
(⁸· **d**   ) of flying from childhood. That dream came true in
1973, when she got her (⁹· **w**   ). After that, she broke many
(¹⁰· **b**   ), becoming the first woman to fly a (¹¹· **t**   )
fighter jet and the first to (¹²· **c**   ) a squadron. She inspired
a generation of young women, opening the (¹³· **c**   ) (¹⁴· **d**   )
and leaving it open for other women to follow.

E Discussion: Share your ideas and opinions with your classmates.

1. What do you know about the U.S. Navy? See what you can find out about their recruiting practices. What is the ratio of male to female recruits?

2. What are some of the advantages of a career in the military?

3. Look for other stories about women who broke barriers and inspired others.

　たとえば, tell him /tel hɪm/ では, /h/ が脱落して /telɪm/ になるため,「テレ（リ）ム」に聞こえることがある。この様に, アクセントのない人称代名詞の he, him, his, her や助動詞 have, has, had などの語頭の /h/ は, 脱落したりごく弱くにしか発音されないことが多い。

— Her father, an Air Force pilot, died in a plane crash when she was
　　just three, but that didn't stop ***her***.　　　　*(Legacy of Captain Mariner, p.3)*

　上の例では, stop her の her /hɚ/ の /h/ 音が脱落して /stɑpɚ/ と発音されているため「スタッパ」のように聞こえる。ただし、"h" で始まるこれらの語が, 文や節の冒頭に来る場合には /h/ 音は脱落しない。この例でも文頭 Her father の /h/ はしっかり発音されている。

— ..., former Vice President Joe Biden's camp is firing back at the
　　President for ***his*** tweet?　　　　　　　　　　　*(Sumo Diplomacy, p.21)*
— ... and the increasing tensions between the president and ***his***
　　political foes over developments at the border.
　　　　　　　　　　　　　　　　　　　　　　　(Mayors Challenge Trump, p.75)
— ..., catching some on ***his*** own team off guard.
　　　　　　　　　　　　　　　　　　　　　　　(Mayors Challenge Trump, p.75)
— ... shelling out $500,000 to consultant Rick Singer, along with ***her***
　　fashion designer husband, ...　　　　*(College Scandal Shock Waves, p.90)*
— The star of *Desperate Housewives* so desperate to land ***her*** daughter
　　in a top school, ...　　　　　　　　　*(College Scandal Shock Waves, p.90)*

News Story 2

America Strong: Foster Grandparents

Air Date: February 16, 2019
Duration: 1′ 47″

Before You Watch the News

Preview Questions

1. What new role do elderly Americans have in some schools?
——年配のアメリカ人たちは学校でどのような役割を担っていますか。

2. How do they feel about it?
——彼らはそのことについてどう感じていますか。

Warm-up Exercises

A Vocabulary Check: Choose the correct definition for each of the words below.

1. spoil (　　)

2. bunch (　　)

3. nurture (　　)

4. stipend (　　)

5. priceless (　　)

a. to care for; to encourage the development of

b. precious; of great value

c. a group of people

d. salary or allowance

e. to pamper; to be overly indulgent

B Fill in the blanks with appropriate expressions from the Vocabulary Check above. Change the word form where necessary.

1. Although they lost their parents at a young age, the twins were ( ) by their loving grandparents.

2. A ( ) of friends are going out for pizza tonight. Want to come?

3. You should really take that trip to Greece you've been talking about. The memories would be ( ).

4. The students were given a small ( ) for helping their professor gather data for her research project.

5. Look at that expensive bag! Kerry's parents really ( ) her since her sister went away to college.

News Story [1′ 47″]

T. Llamas: Finally tonight, "America Strong." We don't have to tell you about the importance of grandparents. But now, something new. Schools making sure **1.** _____

_____

_____. Here's ABC's Karen Travers.

5

K. Travers: At Ludlow-Taylor Elementary School in Washington, D.C., Clementine Bates is called "Grandma."

10

C. Bates: You know how much 8 and 5 is?

K. Travers: Warm, funny, and incredibly energetic, Bates is **2.** _____

_____.

C. Bates: Sometimes I come in in the morning, I say, "I haven't had a hug all day," and they come running to me.

15

Foster grandmother: Two!

K. Travers: The Foster Grandparent Program is nationwide, using people like

Clementine who is 95.

C. Bates: Fifty-nine going on 95.

K. Travers: They bring ³· _____

_____ to

the classroom, something special.

C. Bates: A lot of kids, I think they need love. To me that's one of the most
important things is love.

M. Johnson, teacher: I think she spoils them a little more than I do. I'm the
tough one in the bunch. But she gives that, you know, that nurturing
touch.

Foster grandfather: Take your time.

K. Travers: Foster grandparents are placed in schools ⁴· _____

_____.

Do you often see students in the neighborhood?

C. Bates: Oh, yes, yes. And sometimes I …they say, "Oh, there's Grandma!
There's Grandma! "

School Official: The more role models that our students have both in this
building and when they leave this building, the more confident they are
in moving forward.

K. Travers: The seniors get a small stipend. But the connection they say they
make with the students, the energy they get, that's priceless.

C. Bates: If I wasn't doing this, I would just…I'd be lost.

K. Travers: Lost, and she says,⁵· _____

_____. Karen Travers, ABC News,
Washington.

T. Llamas: So tonight we salute those foster grandparents and all the
grandparents out there. We thank Karen for that story. We thank you
for watching. I'm Tom Llamas in New York. *GMA* and *This Week* in the
morning. I'll see you right back here tomorrow night. Have a great
evening.

Notes
Foster Grandparent Program「フォスター（養育）祖父母プログラム〈国家によるボランティアプログラムとして 1965 年から現在に至るまで全米で実施されている。もともと，低所得層の高齢者への雇用対策として考案された制度で，スタイペンド（stipend）という 1 時間ごとの奨励金が支給される有償のボランティア活動）」　Fifty-nine going on 95.「59 歳で，もうすぐ 95 歳よ〈自分が気も若く元気なので，冗談めかして言っている。逆に，大人びた子どもは，早熟なことをからかわれると "10 going on 35" などと切り返すことがある〉」

After　You Watch the News

Exercises

A Listen to the CD and fill in the blanks in the text.　◎ CD 05

B Mark the following sentences true (T) or false (F) according to the information in the news story.

(　) **1.** Foster grandparents bring love and hugs to the classrooms.

(　) **2.** The program is only running in a few states right now.

(　) **3.** The foster grandparent program depends on volunteers.

(　) **4.** Foster grandparents work in their own neighborhoods.

(　) **5.** Clementine is stricter than the real teachers.

(　) **6.** Some foster grandparents say that the relationships with the children are more important than the stipends.

C Translate the following Japanese into English. Then listen to the CD and practice the conversation with your partner.　◎ CD 06

A: I'm home, Mommy.

B: How was school today, Lily?

A: It was great! Guess what? ¹·_____.

B: Grandma? But your grandma lives out in California.

A: Not that grandma. The grandma we meet in the supermarket sometimes.
²·_____.

B: Well, isn't that kind of her. ³·_____
_____.

A: Our teacher said she's gonna come every week. All the kids are really happy!

1. おばあちゃんが私のクラスに来てみんなにハグしてくれたよ。

2. スペリングや算数を手伝ってくれるよ。

3. そのようなすてきなお手伝いさんが来てくれるなんて，ラッキーなクラスね。

D Summary Practice: Fill in the blanks with suitable words beginning with the letters indicated. ◎ CD 07

Clementine Bates, a (¹· **n**   )-(²· **f**   )-year-old who jokes about her age, is taking part in a new program aiming to connect the
(³· **y**   ) with the (⁴· **w**   ). She is a (⁵· **f**   )
(⁶· **g**   ) at an (⁷· **e**   ) school in Washington, D.C. Clementine is (⁸· **b**   ) by the children, showering them with (⁹· **h**   ) and helping them with their school work. She says the students are excited to see her when they meet in the
(¹⁰· **n**   ) outside of school. Although the
(¹¹· **s**   ) receive a small (¹²· **s**   ) from the schools, they say they would feel (¹³· **l**   ) and (¹⁴· **l**   ) without their young friends. What a win-win situation!

E Discussion: Share your ideas and opinions with your classmates.

1. See if you can find information about other programs that use the talents of senior citizens. Share the information with your classmates.

2. Are there any roles for parents or community members in elementary schools in Japan? Are there any special qualifications? Are they volunteer programs or do the schools pay a stipend?

Assault Weapons Ban in New Zealand

Before You Watch the News

Air Date: March 21, 2019
Duration: 1′ 30″

Preview Questions

1. Why is New Zealand in the news?
　——ニュージーランドがニュースになっているのはなぜですか。

2. What is the reaction in the U.S.?
　——アメリカではどのような反応ですか。

Warm-up Exercises

A Vocabulary Check: Choose the correct definition for each of the words below.

1. mass （　）

2. emerge （　）

3. steely （　）

4. swift （　）

5. advocate （　）

a. a person who publicly supports a particular cause

b. relating to large numbers of people or things

c. hard; determined

d. quick; rapid

e. to come into view; to be seen as

B Fill in the blanks with appropriate expressions from the Vocabulary
Check above. Change the word form where necessary.

1. So far, no clear leader has (   ) from among the 12
   candidates.
2. If Jan succeeds in becoming a nurse, she intends to be an
   (   ) for patients' rights.
3. The witness described her assailant's wavy hair and (   )
   eyes.
4. That young designer's clothes are said to have (   ) appeal.
5. The residents praised the (   ) action of the first responders.

News Story [1′ 30″]

D. Muir: Next tonight, to New Zealand.
   Six days now after that mass
   shooting, killing 50 people, the
   prime minister making good on a
   promise. ¹. _____

   _____

   _____ here at home after
so many mass shootings here in the U.S. Here's ABC's Terry Moran.

T. Moran: As her nation reels from the terror attack, New Zealand's Prime
   Minister Jacinda Ardern has emerged as a leader of stirring sympathy   10
   and steely resolve, announcing a ban on all military-style
   semiautomatics, including assault rifles and high-capacity magazines.

J. Ardern, Prime Minister of New Zealand: The time for the mass and
   2. _____

   must end.   15

T. Moran: New Zealand's swift response has many pro-gun control Americans
   wondering why nothing has happened here.

   There were 20 mass shootings in America last year alone, including
   Parkland, the massacre at Marjory Stoneman Douglas High School,
   3. _____, including   20
   Joaquin Oliver. His father Manuel saying today:

M. Oliver, father of J. Oliver: New
   Zealand is doing the right thing.
   Apparently, we are somehow
   surprised about what New Zealand
   did instead of being surprised
   about what we don't do.

T. Moran: Gun rights advocates here say there are big differences. The Second
   Amendment protects Americans' individual right to own firearms, and
   guns are ⁴· _____
   _____.

   No comment from the White House tonight about those new New
   Zealand laws. The Trump administration did ban bump stocks after that
   Las Vegas shooting. They've made some minor improvements to the
   background checks. But ⁵· _____
   _____ has gone nowhere. David?

D. Muir: Terry Moran tonight. Terry, thank you.

Notes **making good on ~**「（約束）を守る（遂行する）」 **Jacinda Ardern**「ジャシンダ・アーダーン〈2017
年10月より第40代ニュージーランド首相〉」 **stirring sympathy**「溢れんばかりの思いやりの気持ち」
resolve「決意」 **military-style semiautomatics**「軍用半自動小銃；軍隊仕様の半自動式銃〈装填
のみが自動で，発射は一発ずつ手動で引き金を引く軍用銃〉」 **assault rifles**「アサルトライフル；突
撃銃（ライフル）〈戦闘時に兵士が用いるような殺傷力の高い自動小銃や半自動式ライフルなどの総称〉」
high-capacity magazines「大容量弾倉小銃」 **pro-gun control**「銃規制賛成（派）の；銃規制を
訴える（支持する）」 **Parkland**「パークランドの事件〈2018年2月14日，フロリダ州・パークラン
ドのマージョリー・ストーンマン・ダグラス高等学校で発生した銃乱射事件〉」 **Second Amendment**
「憲法修正第2条〈個人が銃器を保有・所持する権利を保障している〉」 **firearms**「銃器」 **bump
stocks**「バンプ・ストック；銃の連射装置〈この装置を取りつけると，自動小銃と同じように立て続
けに速射できるようになる〉」 **Las Vegas shooting**「ラスベガス銃乱射事件〈2017年10月1日に
ラスベガスで発生した銃乱射事件で，58人が犠牲になった〉」 **background checks**「身元調査（確認）；
素性調査」 **gone nowhere**「足踏み状態である；行き詰まる；全く進歩がない；暗礁に乗り上げた」

After You Watch the News

Exercises

A Listen to the CD and fill in the blanks in the text.

◎ CD 08

B Multiple Choice Questions

1. Following the terror attack in New Zealand, the prime minister
   a. showed determination but a lack of sympathy.
   b. responded to the situation quickly and strongly.
   c. urged the president of the U.S. to follow her example.

2. New Zealand and the U.S.
   a. are both home to many strong gun rights advocates.
   b. responded similarly following recent mass shootings.
   c. have different laws and cultures regarding gun violence and gun ownership.

3. What is Manuel Oliver referring to when he says, "New Zealand is doing the right thing"?
   a. There are few violent incidents in the country.
   b. They are making strict laws against owning weapons.
   c. They have elected a female prime minister.

4. In the U.S.
   a. pro-gun control supporters are critical of Jacinda Ardern.
   b. there were 20 mass shootings in schools during the past year.
   c. only minor changes in gun laws have been made by the Trump administration.

C Translate the following Japanese into English. Then listen to the CD and practice the conversation with your partner. ⊙ CD 09

A: Chris, you had a homestay in New Zealand last year. Is your host family okay?

B: Nobody was hurt, ¹· but_____.

A: It was really horrifying. But Prime Minister Ardern is emerging as a truly great leader.

B: She really is! ²· _____

_____.

A: The U.S. should learn from her example.

B: Well, that's not so easy. ³· _____

_____.

A: We'll see what the White House has to say after Prime Minister Ardern's announcement.

1. でも，街中が襲撃で動揺しているようです。
2. 彼女は，攻撃用武器を禁止する約束を守るだろうと，みんなが信じています。
3. 憲法修正第２条が，アメリカ人に銃所持の権利を与えています。

D Summary Practice: Fill in the blanks with suitable words beginning with the letters indicated. ⊙ CD 10

Six days ago New Zealand joined the U.S. as the site of a horrific
(¹· **m**   ) (²· **s**   ). As a result of the terror attack, which killed (³· **f**   ) people, Prime Minister (⁴· **J**   )
(⁵· **A**   ) has shown herself to be a leader full of
(⁶· **s**   ) for those reeling from the incident and
(⁷· **s**   ) resolve to prevent it from happening again. She has announced a ban on all (⁸· **m**   )-(⁹· **s**   )
(¹⁰· **s**   ) — a response that has many Americans wondering why the U.S. is so slow to act on gun violence. The father of one of the victims of last year's (¹¹· **m**   ) at Marjory Stoneman Douglas (¹²· **H**   ) (¹³· **S**   ) is among those who are speaking out. It's true that guns are embedded in American
(¹⁴· **c**   ), but with (¹⁵· **t**   ) mass shootings last year alone, the minor changes made by the Trump
(¹⁶· **a**   ) might not be enough.

16

E Discussion: Share your ideas and opinions with your classmates.

1. The mass shooting of 50 people in their country came as a shock to New Zealand and to the world. See what you can find out about the incident. Look for an update on how gun laws have changed since the attack.

2. Gun violence is a huge problem in the U.S. Look for information on the two sides of the gun debate. The Second Amendment to the Constitution is mentioned in this news story. What does it say? What does that mean for American society today?

3. What is the situation regarding gun ownership and gun violence in Japan?

Useful Grammar from the News　①現在完了形の利用

　テレビニュースは最近起きた（過去の）出来事を報道するものの，その出来事は現在と何らかのつながりがあることがほとんどである。そのため，「事実が明らかになる過程にあることがら」や「過去から継続して起きている問題」について説明したり，「今まさに…している」といった意味を強調する場合，現在完了形が使われる。

— …, New Zealand's Prime Minister Jacinda Ardern ***has emerged*** as a leader of stirring sympathy and steely resolve,…

(Assault Weapons Ban in New Zealand, p.13)

　たとえば，上の例では「ニュージーランドのジャシンダ・アーダーン首相が，溢れんばかりの思いやりの気持ちと断固たる決意を持ったリーダーとして世に出た」とあるが，現時点でもその状態が変わらないことを意味している。

— New Zealand's swift response has many pro-gun control Americans wondering why nothing ***has happened*** here.

(Assault Weapons Ban in New Zealand, p.13)

　さらに，「ニュージーランドでは迅速な対応策がとられたものの，銃規制に賛成するアメリカ人は，なぜアメリカでは何も変わらないのだろうと不思議に思っている」と，ここでも現在完了形が使われている。現在完了形で，現時点でもそ

の状態が変わらないことを示している。

— Something that the Navy **has never done**.
(Legacy of Captain Mariner, p.2)
— But now, we **have learned** authorities feared they were just
minutes from collapsing. *(Notre Dame Cathedral: Full Damage Revealed, p.39)*
— ...*The Hunchback of Notre Dame* **has now shot** up to the top of the
bestseller list here in France.
(Notre Dame Cathedral: Full Damage Revealed, p.40)
— ..., 87% of the glaciers here are receding, creating more open water,
which **has actually helped** grow the humpback population.
(Journey to the Edge, p.51)
— During two days of hearings on Capitol Hill, Trump's education
secretary, Betsy Devos, **has been skewered**.
(Special Olympics Funding, p.56)
— This is funding I **have fought** for behind the scenes for the last
several years. *(Special Olympics Funding, p.57)*
— An ABC News investigation found Columbine may **have inspired**...
(Columbine: 20 Years Later, p.83)
— ..., the survivors and the students **have tried** to make this day...
(Columbine: 20 Years Later, p.84)

Sumo Diplomacy

Before You Watch the News

Air Date: May 26, 2019
Duration: 2' 49"

Preview Questions

1. What happened during President Trump's visit to Tokyo?
——トランプ大統領が日本を訪問中に何が起こりましたか。

2. What was the source of disagreement between the leaders of Japan and the U.S.?
——日米首脳間の意見の不一致の原因は何ですか。

Warm-up Exercises

A Vocabulary Check: Choose the correct definition for each of the words below.

1. foe (   )   **a.** extravagant; excessive

2. lavish (   )   **b.** to spoil; to pamper

3. indulge (   )   **c.** to challenge or weaken

4. discord (   )   **d.** disagreement; conflict

5. undermine (   )   **e.** enemy or rival

B Fill in the blanks with appropriate expressions from the Vocabulary Check above. Change the word form where necessary.

1. Mom and her sisters prepared a (   ) feast for Thanksgiving.

2. The young politician is said to have many fans and no (   ).

3. It's great that Chip has strong opinions, but he should be careful not to (   ) the group's plans.

4. How nice that your grandchildren are coming to visit! Don't (   ) them too much.

5. There seems to be some (   ) among the new club members. Let's have a meeting.

News Story [2' 49"]

T. Llamas: Overseas now from Japan tonight, President Trump with a full schedule of activities that were close to his heart. A round of golf with Prime Minister Abe, who tweeted this selfie from the links, then awarding the President's Cup trophy to [1.] _____. But the president still found time to tweet warm words for North Korea's Kim Jong-un and nasty ones to 2020 foe, former Vice President Joe Biden. ABC White House correspondent Tara Palmeri reporting from Tokyo.

5

10

T. Palmeri: The president getting a lavish layout from the Japanese, catered to indulge "Trump the showman." A ringside seat at a championship sumo match. The president and first lady watching the intense matches.

15

President D. Trump: As sumo grand champion, [2.] _____ _____ the United States President's Cup.

T. Palmeri: Trump awarding a massive 70-pound trophy to the winner. And it didn't end with sumo diplomacy. Japanese Prime Minister Shinzo Abe [3.] _____. The two posing for a selfie before having cheeseburgers with imported U.S. beef, perhaps a nod to

20

progress on a U.S. trade deal.

President D. Trump: The prime minister and I talked a lot today about trade and military and various other things. I think we had a very productive day.

5

T. Palmeri: But looming over the glamour of the visit, a growing discord over North Korea's recent missile tests. Both the Japanese prime minister and National Security Adviser John Bolton saying [4] _____ _____ a UN security resolution. 10 The president then undermined both in this tweet: "North Korea fired off some small weapons, which disturbed some of my people, and others, but not me. I have confidence that Chairman Kim will keep his promise to me, and also smiled when he called Swampman Joe Biden a low IQ individual, and worse. Perhaps that's sending me a signal?" 15

C. Dodd, host "Meet the Press": Can you explain [5] _____

_____ that the president of the United States is essentially siding with a murderous authoritarian dictator over a former vice president in the United States? 20

S. Sanders, White House Press Secretary: Chuck, the president's not siding with that, but I think they agree in their assessment of former Vice President Joe Biden.

T. Palmeri: But even Republican allies in the Senate saying they are troubled by Kim's recent actions. 25

Senator J. Ernst (Republican), Iowa: I find them very disturbing and certainly wouldn't trust Kim Jong-un, so I think [6] _____ _____.

T. Llamas: Tara Palmeri joins us now from Tokyo where she is traveling with the president. And Tara, former Vice President Joe Biden's camp is firing 30 back at the president for his tweet?

T. Palmeri: Tom, an aide for Biden is slamming President Trump for amplifying the dictator's attack on the vice president, calling the tweet "erratic" and "unhinged." Now, Tom, it's extremely rare for a president *7.* _____ on foreign soil.

T. Llamas: Tara Palmeri reporting for us tonight from Tokyo.

5

Notes **close to his heart**「とても大切な（大事な・重要な）こと」 **nasty ones**「ひどい発言〈トランプ大統領は，訪問中の東京で記者会見した際，北朝鮮がバイデン氏を「IQ の低い人物」と呼んだことについて，自分も同意見だと発言した〉」 **layout**「おもてなし（計画）」 **catered to ~**「~のために用意された」 **the showman**「（外交政策の）ショーマン〈トランプ大統領は頻繁にツイッターで情報を発信する。G 20 大阪サミットの終了日の 2019 年 6 月 29 日に "I will be leaving Japan for South Korea (with President Moon). While there, if Chairman Kim of North Korea sees this, I would meet him at the Border/DMZ just to shake his hand and say Hello(?)!" と金正恩委員長に会談を呼びかけた結果，南北の軍事境界線での会談が現実となった。全世界が「トランプ劇場」を見守る事になり，まさにトランプ大統領は外交政策のショーマンである〉」 **ringside seat**「土俵に近い席（升席）〈土俵近くの升席に椅子を置いて観戦した〉」 **championship sumo match**「大相撲（夏場所）」 **intense matches**「熱戦」 **United States President's Cup**「アメリカ合衆国大統領杯」 **massive**「巨大な；非常に重い」 **nod to ~**「~に賛成する（合図）；~に同意する」 **trade deal**「貿易協定；通商問題〈トランプ大統領は日米貿易不均衡の是正に強い姿勢を示していたとされる〉」 **looming over ~**「~に（暗い）陰を落としているのは」 **glamour**「華やかさ」 **National Security Adviser John Bolton**「ジョン・ボルトン国家安全保障問題担当顧問（大統領補佐官）」 **UN security resolution**「国連安保理決議〈ボルトン補佐官は北朝鮮の短距離弾道ミサイルの発射実験を国連制裁決議違反として批判していた〉」 **disturbed some of my people, and others**「私の政権当局者の一部などは懸念を抱いたが」 **Swampman**「スワンプマン；ヘドロ男〈swamp（沼）は長年政治家を務めてきた人を批判する表現〉」 **a low IQ individual, and worse**「IQ が低いか，もっとひどい男」 **that's sending me a signal?**「恐らく私へのシグナルではないか？〈北朝鮮国営の朝鮮中央通信は，2020 年米大統領選への出馬を表明している民主党のバイデン前副大統領を「ヘドロ男」や「IQ の低い愚か者」などと酷評したことを，金正恩（キムジョンウン）朝鮮労働党委員長が自分を支持する（正恩氏と交渉できるのはバイデン氏ではなく自分であるという）シグナルではないかと喜んだ〉」 **siding with ~ over...**「…より~側につく；…より~に味方する」 **murderous authoritarian dictator**「残忍で権威主義的な独裁者」 **Republican allies**「共和党の盟友（議員たち）」 **the Senate**「上院」 **disturbing**「憂慮すべき；不穏な（動き）」 **firing back at ~**「~に対して反撃に出る」 **slamming**「（厳しく）非難する」 **amplifying**「増幅する〈トランプ大統領のツイートが，金委員長のバイデン前副大統領に対する批判を増幅することになった〉」 **erratic**「場当たり的」 **unhinged**「常軌を逸している」 **on foreign soil**「異国の地で」

Background of the News

　トランプ大統領が 2019 年 5 月に訪日した際，まず安倍首相がゴルフ接待，昼食には米国産牛肉を使ったチーズバーガー，夕方は東京・両国の国技館に招待するという盛大なおもてなし（lavish layout）で迎えた。国技館では升席 4 升分にソファ椅子が据えられ，周囲を警護にあたるダークスーツの SP らがガードする中での観戦になった。100 人を超える SP や警察官が，国技館で厳重な警備態勢をとったという。トランプ大統領が寄贈した「アメリカ合衆国大統領杯」（President's Cup trophy）は，賜杯よりさらに一回り大きい。この「トランプ杯」の表彰は 5 月の夏場所に限定して今後も続けられる。

　北朝鮮は 2019 年 5 月，日本海に向けて短距離弾道ミサイルを発射したが，トランプ大統領は米国を脅かさない短距離ならば事実上，容認する考えを示し，ボルトン国家安全保障問題担当顧問（National Security Adviser John Bolton）ら側近たちや日本政府と意見の不一致（discord）を示した。トランプ大統領は自国第一主義（America first）を標榜しているので，日本を射程に含む中距離ミサイルもトランプ大統領が黙認することが懸念される。北朝鮮は国連安保理決議（UN security resolution）でミサイルの発射を禁じられているため，これに違反することになる。

　2019 年 6 月には，トランプ大統領の呼びかけで，現職の米大統領として初めて南北の軍事境界線を越えて金正恩氏との電撃的な会談が実現した。これも（外交政策の）ショーマン（the showman）トランプ大統領のパフォーマンス外交のひとつである。

After　You Watch the News

Exercises

A Listen to the CD and fill in the blanks in the text.　　 CD 11

B Multiple Choice Questions

1. In what ways did the Japanese indulge the U.S. president during his visit?
   a. by serving American food
   b. by letting him play in a sumo match
   c. by letting him win his golf game with Prime Minister Abe

2. What *DIDN'T* President Trump do while he was in Japan?

    a. pose for a selfie and eat cheeseburgers with the Japanese prime minister

    b. praise the North Korean leader and criticize the former U.S. vice president

    c. tweet a photo of himself with Prime Minister Abe

3. Which of the following statements is true about both Trump and Abe?

    a. They are both distrustful of the North Korean leader.

    b. They are both trying to make progress on a trade deal.

    c. They are both known to attack their political rivals when overseas.

4. Who openly disagreed with President Trump's attitude towards Chairman Kim?

    a. Joe Biden and Senator Ernst

    b. Sarah Sanders and the president's wife

    c. both *a* and *b*

C **Translate the following Japanese into English. Then listen to the CD and practice the conversation with your partner.** ◉ CD 12

A: I'm so psyched about my trip to Japan next month!

B: You'll have a great time. ¹· _____

_____?

A: Well, I'm hoping to catch a high school baseball game. ²· _____

_____

_____.

B: No sumo?

A: No way! It's way too expensive. Oh — and I'm planning to eat a lot of great sushi.

B: No cheeseburgers?

A: Very funny! ³· _____

_____.

1. 何を一番楽しみにしていますか。

2. 滞在中に大きなトーナメントが開催されるのです。

3. 日本に行ってアメリカの食べ物を食べるのはトランプ大統領ぐらいです。

D Summary Practice: Fill in the blanks with suitable words beginning with the letters indicated.　　　　　　　　　○ CD 13

U.S. President Donald Trump has many special memories from his recent trip to Tokyo. In addition to posing for (¹· **s**　　　) with the Japanese (²· **p**　　) (³· **m**　　　　) on the (⁴· **g**　) course, he also had the honor of awarding a (⁵· **m**　　　　) trophy to the sumo (⁶· **g**　　　) (⁷· **c**　　　　　). But it wasn't all sports and cheeseburgers. The two leaders also engaged in serious talks about (⁸· **t**　　　) and the (⁹· **m**　　　　). One subject that cast a shadow over the otherwise (¹⁰· **l**　　　　　) welcome was the topic of North Korea's (¹¹· **m**　　　) (¹²· **t**　　　). While Abe agrees with the U.S. (¹³· **N**　　　) (¹⁴· **S**　　　　) Adviser that the tests (¹⁵· **v**　　　　) a UN (¹⁶· **s**　　　　) (¹⁷· **r**　　　　　　), President Trump (¹⁸· **t**　　　　) his support for Chairman Kim and his confidence that the chairman will keep his (¹⁹· **p**　　　). Trump was also pleased with the North Korean leader's insulting comments about his (²⁰· **f**　), former (²¹· **v**　　) (²²· **p**　　　　　) Joe Biden. Trump is showing that he can stir up controversy whether at home or when traveling (²³· **o**　　　　).

E Discussion: Share your ideas and opinions with your classmates.

1. How much do you know about the relationship between Donald Trump and Shinzo Abe? Check the Internet and see what you can find out. How many times have they met in person?
2. Trade is mentioned in this news story. What products are traded between the U.S. and Japan? Is it a balanced trade deal? How has the situation changed over the past ten years?
3. While the U.S. president was in Japan he played golf and enjoyed a sumo match. If you were in charge of hosting a foreign guest, what other activities might you consider?

　一般的に，フォーマルな書き言葉では and, but, so などの接続詞を文頭に使うのは避けられる。論文などの文中にこれらを文頭に置くと，口語的で幼稚な印象を与えるからである。ニュース英語では口語的なスタイルが好まれるため，特に否定の意味を強調する際には，文頭に but が使われる。

— ***But*** looming over the glamour of the visit, a growing discord over
　　North Korea's recent missile tests. 　　　　　　　　　　*(Sumo Diplomacy, p.21)*

　上記の例では，現地東京からリポートしている記者は，東京での安倍首相との会談の成果を伝えるトランプ大統領のスピーチに対して，実際は北朝鮮のミサイル発射実験で不安が高まっている事実を強調するために but を文頭においている。

— ***And*** Tara, former Vice President Joe Biden's camp is firing back at
　　the President for his tweet? 　　　　　　　　　　　　　*(Sumo Diplomacy, p.21)*
— ***So*** tonight, we honor the legacy of Captain Mariner.
　　　　　　　　　　　　　　　　　　　　　　　(Legacy of Captain Mariner, p.3)
— ***But*** now, something new. 　　　*(America Strong: Foster Grandparents, p.8)*
— ***And*** this evening, the young American woman who left the U.S. to
　　marry ISIS fighters. 　　　　　　　　　　　　　　　*(American ISIS Bride, p.28)*
— ***But*** now, we have learned authorities feared they were just minutes
　　from collapsing. 　　　　　*(Notre Dame Cathedral: Full Damage Revealed, p.39)*
— ***So*** this is the whole point of this mission, to get as close as possible
　　to these whales... 　　　　　　　　　　　　　　　　　*(Journey to the Edge, p.50)*
— ***But*** it comes after lawmakers from both parties made it very clear...
　　　　　　　　　　　　　　　　　　　　　　　(Special Olympics Funding, p.57)
— ***And*** outside the Hanoi Hilton today, the men of Foxtrot 21.
　　　　　　　　　　　　　　　　　　　　　　(American Heroes in Vietnam, p.62)

American ISIS Bride

Before You Watch the News

Air Date: February 18, 2019
Duration: 1′ 49″

Preview Questions

1. How did foreign women end up in Syria?
——外国人女性はシリアでどのような目にあいましたか。

2. What is their situation now?
——彼女たちの現状はどのような状態ですか。

Warm-up Exercises

A Vocabulary Check: Choose the correct definition for each of the words below.

1. plea （ 　 ）
2. claim （ 　 ）
3. propaganda （ 　 ）
4. widow （ 　 ）
5. lure （ 　 ）

a. to tempt someone to do something or go somewhere
b. an emotional request; an appeal
c. to declare to be one's own property or area
d. a woman whose husband has died
e. promotional information, usually biased

B Fill in the blanks with appropriate expressions from the Vocabulary Check above. Change the word form where necessary.

1. The little boy was (   ) into a car, but he managed to escape.

2. Nell became a (   ) at a young age, when her husband was killed in the war.

3. Our neighbors tried to (   ) the pond between our houses, but the deed showed that it belonged to us.

4. How can you listen to that (   )? You know that TV channel is famous for misleading stories.

5. When they heard their (   ) for assistance, many people chipped in to help the flood victims.

News Story [1′ 49″]

D. Muir: Now to our team inside Syria again tonight. And this evening, the young American woman who left the U.S. to marry ISIS fighters. She had a baby boy. And tonight, her plea, **1.** _____

_____

_____. And it comes just as the U.S. now takes back that territory that had been claimed by ISIS in Syria. ABC's James Longman from inside that country again tonight.

J. Longman: Tonight, as the ISIS veil is stripped away, this young American mother is pleading to come home.

H. Muthana, mother: I realized I've made a big mistake and I know I've ruined my future and my son's future and I deeply, deeply regret it.

J. Longman: Hoda Muthana, here with her 18-month son, left Alabama to marry an ISIS fighter four years ago. **2.** _____.

She spread ISIS propaganda online, calling for attacks on Americans. Now, she tells *The Guardian*, after trying to escape, **3.** _____

_____.

H. Muthana: From what I heard, if they, if they were to read my messages, I would have been killed.

J. Longman: Muthana married three times during her time here, each time to an ISIS fighter. Each time made a widow. Muthana is not the only woman lured by the terror group. There are 1,500 ^{4.} _____

_____ .   5

Nineteen-year-old Shamima Begum from London is one of them. She just   10
gave birth to her third child. The first two, she claims, dead.

S. Begum: At first, it was nice. It was like how they, you know, showed it in the videos.

J. Longman: She described life in the Islamic State, including watching
beheadings.   15

S. Begum: I knew about those things. And I was, I was okay with it.

J. Longman: But now, ^{5.} _____

_____ .

S. Begum: I don't wanna take care of my child in this camp, because I'm afraid
he might even die in this camp.   20

J. Longman: The British will not bring Begum back. While, as an American,
Muthana can expect to be brought home to face justice. ^{6.} _____

_____

_____ to follow the U.S. lead. David?

D. Muir: All right, James Longman and our team inside Syria for days now.   25
Our thanks to you.

Notes **ISIS**「アイシス；イスラム国〈中東のイラク，シリアの周辺地域で活動するイスラム過激派組織イラクとシリアのイスラム国（Islamic State of Iraq and Syria）の略称。国（state）と名乗ってはいるが，これは自称であり，イスラム国を国家として承認した国はない〉」 **ISIS veil is stripped away**「アイシスのベールを外して〈アイシスの支配地域に暮らすイスラム教徒の女性は，常に全身を覆うブルカと呼ばれる黒い衣装をまとっている。今回，顔を覆うベールを外してインタビューに応じた〉」 ***The Guardian***「ガーディアン〈イギリス大手の新聞〉」 **Islamic State**「イスラム国」 **beheadings**「斬首」 **face justice**「法の裁きを受ける；正当な裁判を受ける」 **lead**「先例」

シャミマ・ベガム（Shamima Begum）さんは，2015年に15歳で英国からシリアに渡航し，イスラム過激派組織「イスラム国」(ISIS) に参加した。オランダ人戦闘員と結婚後，子供2人は病気と栄養失調で死亡したが，シリア東部の難民キャンプで新たに生まれた男児のために英国に帰りたいと，英国メディアに訴えていた。しかし，その後，生後3週未満で男児は肺の感染症で死亡した。本ニュースでも報道されているように，英政府はテロ組織に加入した経緯を踏まえ，帰国拒否とベガムさんの市民権を剥奪すると決めたと発表した。すでに英国では，テロ組織に参加した100人以上の市民権を剥奪している。

現在，シリアでのIS掃討作戦は最終段階に入っており，米政府はイスラム国が弱体化したとして米軍をシリアから撤収させる方針である。2012年以降，欧州諸国から約5,000人が戦闘員としてシリアなどに渡ったが，徐々に帰国しており，帰国を認めた国では彼らに法の裁きを受けさせる（face justice）対応をとっている。

After   You Watch the News

Exercises

A Listen to the CD and fill in the blanks in the text.　　　　　◎CD 14

B Multiple Choice Questions

1. ISIS

   a. wants women to leave when their husbands die.

   b. is now losing the land it had claimed in Syria.

   c. has lured a small number of foreign women as brides.

2. Hoda Muthana

   a. spread anti-American propaganda online.

   b. claims to have been okay watching beheadings.

   c. has never dared try to escape from the terror group.

3. Which is true of both Hoda Muthana and Shamima Begum?

    a. They both lost family members in Syria.

    b. They both had hoped to become ISIS fighters.

    c. They will both receive assistance from President Trump.

4. Which of the following will probably happen?

    a. Hoda Muthana will return to the U.S. and be put on trial.

    b. Shamima Begum will return to London with her children.

    c. Neither of the women will ever leave Syria.

C **Translate the following Japanese into English. Then listen to the CD and practice the conversation with your partner.** ⊙ CD 15

A: Did you see Hoda on the news last night?

B: No! Is she back in the States now? I heard her third husband died.

A: That's what they reported. ¹· _____

_____

_____.

B: After spreading anti-American propaganda online? What does the government say?

A: ²· _____

_____. That doesn't sound very good.

B: But it's surely better than staying with ISIS.

A: ³· She said that_____

_____

_____.

B: What a horrible situation.

1. 彼女には今 18 ヶ月の息子がいて，アメリカに帰国したがっています。

2. トランプ大統領は，法の裁きを受けさせるために彼女を帰国させたいと考えています。

3. 自分の身の安全を心配しており，大きな過ちを犯したことを実感していると言いました。

D Summary Practice: Fill in the blanks with suitable words beginning with the letters indicated. ⊙ CD 16

ABC's James Longman is in (¹· S   ) reporting on foreign women who have become the (²· **b**   ) of ISIS (³· **f**   ). One of those women, Hoda Muthana, left her home in (⁴· **A**   ) at the age of (⁵· **n**   ) and has now become a (⁶· **w**   ) three times. The mother of an (⁷· **e**   )-month-old son, she once tried to (⁸· **e**   ) and now fears for her life. In the camp where she lives, (⁹· **f**   ) wives and their children number over one thousand (¹⁰· **f**   ) (¹¹· **h**   ). Among the other young brides is Shamima Begum from (¹²· **L**   ). Two of her children have died and she fears her third baby will not survive either if they remain there. Shamima said that at first, life in the (¹³· **I**   ) state was nice, but she is now (¹⁴· **p**   ) to go home to the U.K. These young women and others like them have deep (¹⁵· **r**   ) about the decisions they made as teens.

E Discussion: Share your ideas and opinions with your classmates.

1. How much do you know about ISIS? Do an Internet search and see what you can learn about this terrorist group. Share your findings with the class.

2. The two foreign women interviewed for this story were very young when they left their home countries to join ISIS. Why do you think they might have made the decision to do so?

Milestone Mission: Virgin Galactic

Before You Watch the News

Air Date: February 22, 2019
Duration: 1' 21"

Preview Questions

1. What milestone was reached by Virgin Galactic?
   ——ヴァージン・ギャラクティック社が成し遂げた画期的な出来事は何ですか。

2. What are they aiming for next?
   ——彼らの次の目標は何ですか。

Warm-up Exercises

A Vocabulary Check: Choose the correct definition for each of the words below.

1. milestone (　)   **a.** height, elevation
2. crew (　)   **b.** to explode
3. blast (　)   **c.** a turning point; an important step
4. deadly (　)   **d.** causing or able to cause death
5. altitude (　)   **e.** a group of people who work on a ship, train or aircraft

B Fill in the blanks with appropriate expressions from the Vocabulary Check above. Change the word form where necessary.

1. The (   ) were happy to talk to the passengers about their experiences on the ship.

2. The guest speaker reminded us that graduation is an important (   ).

3. All parents must keep (   ) weapons locked in a cabinet away from children.

4. It's common to get nose bleeds at high (   ).

5. The construction workers used power tools to (   ) through the several layers of solid rock.

News Story [1′ 21″]

D. Muir: We move on tonight to a new milestone in the mission to put tourists in space. A test passenger made it to space today. Virgin Galactic soaring nearly 56 miles above Earth. The crew taking off from California's Mojave Desert for the first time [1.] _____ _____. Here's David Kerley. 5

Astronaut: Release, release, release. 10

D. Kerley: Virgin Galactic blasting away from its mother ship, making it more than 50 miles above Earth, what the FAA considers space, and this second time, with a passenger. The company's chief astronaut trainer Beth Moses flying in SpaceShipTwo and [2.] _____ _____. That's the back of her head, as she got a sense of what 15 paying passengers will experience. The celebrations after a 14-year effort. Richard Branson's company suffering a deadly crash five years ago.

Astronaut: Check that out. We can see Mexico.

D. Kerley: While Branson will charge [3.] _____ 20

_____ to future space
tourists for four minutes of
weightlessness, he says he's trying
to inspire us.

With altitude, you're trying to
change attitudes.

5

R. Branson, founder, Virgin group: They view the Earth very differently
having been to space and they come back determined to **4.** _____
_____ we live on.

D. Kerley: Richard Branson says he wants to be one of the first to go to space.
He's aiming for this summer, **5.** _____
_____, and his birthday. David?

10

D. Muir: All right, stay tuned. David Kerley, thank you.

Notes　**made it to ~**「～に到達した；～までたどり着いた」　**Mojave Desert**「モハベ砂漠〈カリフォルニア州，ユタ州，ネバダ州，アリゾナ州にまたがる砂漠〉」　**Release**「リリース；切り離し〈ヴァージン・ギャラクティック社の宇宙船スペースシップ２（SpaceShipTwo）は，予定の高度に達した後，母船から切り離され，ロケットエンジンに点火，宇宙空間に向け急上昇した〉」　**Virgin Galactic**「ヴァージン・ギャラクティック社〈英国の大富豪リチャード・ブランソン氏が率いる航空宇宙企業が設立したヴァージン・ギャラクティック社は，民間企業による宇宙旅行事業の実現を目指している〉」　**FAA** = 巻末資料参照　**chief astronaut trainer Beth Moses**「主任宇宙飛行士インストラクターのベス・モーゼスさん」　**SpaceShipTwo**「スペースシップ２〈ヴァージン・ギャラクティック社とその姉妹会社が開発した商用宇宙船〉」　**got a sense of ~**「～（無重力）の感覚を経験した」　**inspire**「（宇宙飛行に対する関心・興味を）かき立てる」

Background of the News

　夢の宇宙旅行時代が間もなく来るのだろうか。日経産業新聞（2019/02/27）によると，英ヴァージングループ創設者のリチャード・ブランソン（Richard Branson）氏が率いる米宇宙旅行会社「ヴァージン・ギャラクティック社」（Virgin Galactic）は，乗客（passenger）を搭乗した状態で初めて宇宙飛行に成功した。ヴァージン・ギャラクティック社は，パイロット以外の乗客が宇宙船に乗って宇宙空間を飛行したのは世界で初めてとしている。

　ヴァージン・ギャラクティック社は，2019年中に上場企業になると発表した。同社は2020年にも一般客を乗せた宇宙旅行サービスを始める計画である。宇宙旅行の料金は1人25万ドル（約2,750万円）で，これにはアメリカでの3日間の準備訓練の費用も含まれる。すでに世界60カ国から600人以上の申し込みがあり，日本からも19名の予約があるという。

　宇宙旅行サービスでは他にも，アマゾンの創業者であるジェフ・ベゾス氏が率いる宇宙開発ベンチャーの「ブルーオリジン社」や，起業家イーロン・マスク氏が私財を投じて設立した「スペースX社」も開発を競っている。また，日本国内ではZOZOの元社長・前澤氏が，2023年予定の月周回旅行を「スペースX社」と契約したことが大きな話題となった。

After　You Watch the News

Exercises

A Listen to the CD and fill in the blanks in the text.　　　◎ CD 17

B Mark the following sentences true (T) or false (F) according to the information in the news story.

(　　) **1.** Today's flight was the second flight into space with a test passenger.

(　　) **2.** The company had a serious accident nine years into their attempt to fly into space.

(　　) **3.** Beth Moses was the pilot of the Virgin Galactic space flight.

(　　) **4.** In the future, space tourists will be charged $250,000 for the trip.

(　　) **5.** Branson claims that people who have been to space care more about the Earth.

(　　) **6.** Branson hopes to travel to space on his 50th birthday.

C Translate the following Japanese into English. Then listen to the CD and practice the conversation with your partner. ⊙ CD 18

A: I heard you're working three jobs now. What's up?

B: I'm saving up for a trip. *¹·*_____.

A: Holy smokes! Where are you planning to go that costs that much?

B: To space! They just sent a space passenger up on the Virgin Galactic. I want to go next. It's my dream.

A: You're crazy! *²·*_____?

B: Yeah, but those problems have been solved now.

   *³·*_____.

A: Well, good luck!

1. 25万ドル貯めなければなりません。

2. 5年前，あの犠牲者を出した飛行のことを覚えていないのですか。

3. リチャード・ブランソン自身，来年の夏に行きたいと願っています。

D Summary Practice: Fill in the blanks with suitable words beginning with the letters indicated. ⊙ CD 19

Founder of the (*¹· **V**_____*) Group, (*²· **R**_____*) (*³· **B**_____*), came one step closer to realizing his (*⁴· **m**_____*) to start sending (*⁵· **t**_____*) to space. The Virgin (*⁶· **G**_____*) took off from the (*⁷· **M**_____*) (*⁸· **D**_____*) and made it over (*⁹· **f**_____*) miles above Earth with passenger Beth Moses on board. There, she floated in (*¹⁰· **z**_____*) (*¹¹· **g**_____*). Future passengers will pay a quarter of a (*¹²· **m**_____*) dollars to do that for (*¹³· **f**_____*) minutes. The (*¹⁴· **m**_____*) was joyfully celebrated, particularly because of a (*¹⁵· **d**_____*) mishap five years ago. Branson himself hopes to be on a flight next summer, which marks the (*¹⁶· **f**_____*) anniversary of the (*¹⁷· **m**_____*) landing.

E Discussion: Share your ideas and opinions with your classmates.

1. Learn more about Richard Branson. What other projects has the entrepreneur been involved with over the years?

2. What has Japan been doing in the field of space travel? Do an Internet search on the Japanese Space Agency and Hayabusa.

Notre Dame Cathedral: Full Damage Revealed

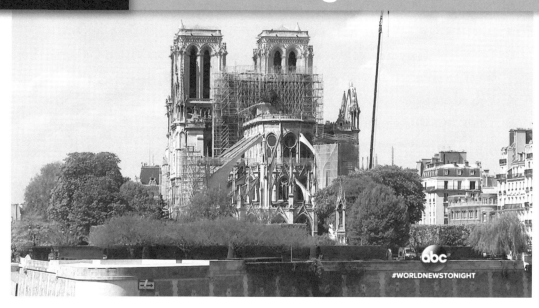

#WORLDNEWSTONIGHT

Before You Watch the News

Air Date: April 17, 2019
Duration: 2′ 01″

Preview Questions

1. What is the extent of the damage done to Notre Dame Cathedral?
　　――ノートルダム寺院の被害はどのような状況ですか。

2. What do authorities fear might happen next?
　　――当局が懸念していることは何ですか。

Warm-up Exercises

A Vocabulary Check: Choose the correct definition for each of the words below.

1. collapse （　）　　　　**a.** unity; mutual support

2. scope （　）　　　　　**b.** extent; range

3. douse （　）　　　　　**c.** to fall down; to crumble

4. solidarity （　）　　　**d.** to repair; to return to a previous state

5. restore （　）　　　　**e.** to soak with liquid; to drench

B **Fill in the blanks with appropriate expressions from the Vocabulary Check above. Change the word form where necessary.**

1. Aunt Peggy was told it would cost a lot of money to (   ) the table to its former condition.

2. In a show of (   ), all of the team members shaved their heads when Tom lost his hair due to his cancer treatment.

3. When he realized he would be caught, the thief (   ) the car with gasoline and set it on fire.

4. The police officer was not willing to reveal the (   ) of the investigation.

5. The children's sand castle (   ) when it was hit by a large wave.

News Story [2′ 01″]

D. Muir: We have new video here of the damage at Notre Dame Cathedral, the view from above tonight showing the roof completely gone there.

The view into the cathedral from the air, **1.** _____

_____.

But now, we have learned authorities feared they were just minutes from collapsing. And ABC's James Longman from Paris again tonight.

J. Longman: New images tonight of Notre Dame revealing the scope of destruction. Its top charred from end to end. Huge sections of the roof collapsed, a hole in France's heart. As teams today doused the building, fresh worry the remaining wood and lead above was weakened by the fire and **2.** _____.

Expert: (Speaking in French)

J. Longman: The head of France's Construction Federation telling us the same materials that once held this building together could now bring it all

down. French officials say Notre
Dame was ^{3.} _____

_____

_____

_____. And tonight, we're
hearing from Father Fournier, the
hero firefighter chaplain who
rushed in to save the relics as the church's spire fell.

Father Fournier, firefighter chaplain: (Speaking in French)

J. Longman: He says his team broke into the area holding the famed Crown of
Thorns believed to have been worn by Jesus. They found a staffer with a
code to quickly unlock its container so they could rush the relic to safety.
Across France today, the sound of solidarity, ^{4.} _____
_____ for their mother church who no
longer can.

D. Muir: And James Longman joins us live tonight from outside the cathedral.
And, James, we know, so far, about a billion dollars has been raised to
restore Notre Dame?

J. Longman: Yes, that's right, but they're probably going to need another
billion to complete the work. President Macron wants this done in five
years, but experts say it's probably gonna take at least twice as long to
rebuild. And, David, ^{5.} _____
_____ that *The Hunchback of Notre Dame* has now shot
up to the top of the bestseller list here in France. David?

D. Muir: Incredible and not terribly surprising. James Longman, our thanks to
you for reporting from Paris again tonight.

Notes from the air「上空からの」 authorities「当局」 charred「焼け焦げた；炭化した；黒焦げになった」
lead「なまり〈大聖堂の屋根や尖塔などに使われていた 300 トンの鉛が, 火事の高熱で溶けて拡散した〉」
Construction Federation「建設連合〈全仏 57,000 社が加盟する建設業団体 (Federation Francais
du Batiment)〉」 bring it all down「すべて崩落する」 Father Fournier「フルニエ神父」
firefighter chaplain「パリ消防旅団お付きの司祭」 relics「聖遺物」 spire「尖塔」 Crown of
Thorns「イバラの冠〈イエス・キリストが処刑を受けるためゴルゴタの丘まで十字架を背負って歩か
された際に, 頭にかぶっていたとされる冠〉」 staffer「職員」 mother church「(本山となる) 母教会」
The Hunchback of Notre Dame「『ノートル゠ダム・ド・パリ』〈フランスの文豪ヴィクトル・ユー
ゴーによる小説〉」 shot up to ~「~に躍り出た；~へと急上昇した」

After   You Watch the News

Exercises

A Listen to the CD and fill in the blanks in the text.   ⊙ CD 20

B Multiple Choice Questions

1. The damage to the cathedral
   a. included the loss of the entire roof and two famous towers.
   b. included the loss of the most famous relics housed there.
   c. could actually have been a great deal worse than it was.

2. One current concern about the cathedral is that
   a. the Crown of Thorns may have been damaged by water.
   b. the fire and water weakened the wood and lead and it could collapse.
   c. the French president insists that the repairs be made within five
        years.

3. Which of the following shows the French love for Notre Dame Cathedral?
   a. the heroic efforts of the firefighters
   b. the sudden popularity of *The Hunchback of Notre Dame*
   c. both of the above

4. The restoration of Notre Dame Cathedral can probably be completed
   a. in five years for one billion dollars.
   b. in five years for two billion dollars.
   c. in ten years for two billion dollars.

C Translate the following Japanese into English. Then listen to the CD and practice the conversation with your partner. CD 21

A: Listen! Can you hear the church bells?

B: Yes. ¹._____

_____.

A: It's really a miracle that no one was killed, isn't it?

B: Indeed. ²._____

_____.

A: And to save the relics!

B: ³._____?

A: It's the heart of Paris. Of course they will.

1. ノートルダムのために団結してフランス中で鐘をならしているのです。
2. 火事を止める努力をした消防士たちは本当のヒーローでした。
3. 寺院を本当に復旧させることができると思いますか。

D Summary Practice: Fill in the blanks with suitable words beginning with the letters indicated. CD 22

As the days go by, Paris and the world are getting a clearer sense of the (¹· s_____) of damage to Notre Dame Cathedral from the recent devastating (²· f____). Videos shot from above show that the entire (³· r____) vanished, although the two iconic (⁴· t_____) remain. (⁵· A_____) have revealed that they, too, were just minutes from (⁶· c_____). There are fresh worries that as the charred building continues to be (⁷· d_____) with water, the remaining wood could be (⁸· w_____) and potentially collapse. In an interview with (⁹· F_____) (¹⁰· F_____), the firefighter (¹¹· c_____), he explained that he and his team rushed into the burning cathedral with the aim of saving the precious (¹²· r_____) housed there. A staffer unlocked the container holding the (¹³· C_____) of (¹⁴· T_____), allowing them to rush it to safety. A (¹⁵· b_____) dollars has been raised already to (¹⁶· r_____) the beloved cathedral, but (¹⁷· e_____) say it could actually cost twice that amount. In the meantime, France has a (¹⁸· h____) in its heart.

E Discussion: Share your ideas and opinions with your classmates.

1. According to the news story, the partial destruction of Notre Dame Cathedral "left a hole in France's heart." What buildings in this country hold such a special place in the hearts of Japanese people?

2. There are numerous YouTube videos available online related to Notre Dame Cathedral. Among them are walking tours, discussions of the Gothic architecture, and video clips of the fire as it was taking place. Choose one that interests you and watch it. Then discuss it with your classmates.

3. Do an Internet search on the Crown of Thorns. Why did it mean so much to save it from being lost in the fire?

Three-year-old Boy Fighting Cancer

Air Date: May 9, 2019
Duration: 1' 15"

Preview Questions

1. What legal battle is playing out in Florida?
——どのような法廷闘争がフロリダで展開されていますか。

2. What is the outcome for now?
——現時点ではどのような結果になっていますか。

Warm-up Exercises

A Vocabulary Check: Choose the correct definition for each of the words below.

1. weigh in （　）   **a.** to experience; to be subjected to

2. tug of war （　）   **b.** different; substitute

3. undergo （　）   **c.** to promise; to swear to do something

4. alternative （　）   **d.** to give one's opinion

5. vow （　）   **e.** a situation in which two groups oppose each other

B Fill in the blanks with appropriate expressions from the Vocabulary Check above. Change the word form where necessary.

1. Because of his bee allergies, my brother has to (   ) a series of injections.
2. We can't make a final decision until the whole team has (   ).
3. As a candidate, the governor (   ) to do more to protect the environment, but he hasn't followed up.
4. The highway is closed temporarily for repairs. We'll have to find an (   ) route.
5. There was a constant (   ) between City Hall and the local residents over the construction of the tower.

News Story [1' 15"]

D. Muir: We turn next tonight here to the three-year-old boy fighting cancer. His parents object to chemotherapy. But tonight, a judge now weighing in,

1. _____

_____.

Here's ABC's Victor Oquendo.

V. Oquendo: The Florida boy at the center of a legal tug of war now ordered to undergo chemotherapy 2. _____

_____.

T. Bland-Ball, mother: This is not about whether we're choosing alternative therapies, natural therapies. This is about our rights as parents to seek other options.

V. Oquendo: The parents of three-year-old Noah McAdams, who was diagnosed with leukemia, took their son to Kentucky for alternative treatments after they say he had violent mood swings from chemotherapy. They claim tests showed his cancer was gone, but police in Florida soon tracked them down and removed Noah from their home. Doctors who treat this cancer say 3. _____

_____.

Dr. B. Shah, Moffitt Cancer Center: We
have no way of saying that he is
cured of leukemia **4.** _____

_____.

V. Oquendo: Noah's parents are vowing
to fight the court's decision.

T. Bland-Ball, mother: There are other options other than chemotherapy. And I
think this really opened up a good discussion on parental rights, about
patient rights.

V. Oquendo: David, the judge ruled **5.** _____

_____, but Noah must undergo 14 more days
of chemotherapy, after which doctors will determine whether his
leukemia is in remission.

5

10

Notes   **chemotherapy**「化学療法」 **mood swings**「気分変動；気分のむら；気分の揺れ」 **tracked them down**「両親を追った」 **in remission**「寛解期に入った」

After   You Watch the News

Exercises

A Listen to the CD and fill in the blanks in the text.   ◉ CD 23

B Mark the following sentences true (T) or false (F) according to the
information in the news story.

(   ) **1.** Noah's parents disagree with the doctors but agree with the judge.

(   ) **2.** According to Dr. Shah, it is impossible to know at this time if the
boy is really cured.

(   ) **3.** Noah's mother claimed her son suffered severe side effects from the
chemotherapy.

(   ) **4.** Noah had new tests following his treatment in Kentucky.

(   ) **5.** The judge ruled that the boy's treatment should continue until his cancer is in remission.

(   ) **6.** Noah was taken away from his parents because the alternative treatment was not working.

C **Translate the following Japanese into English. Then listen to the CD and practice the conversation with your partner.**   CD 24

A: Little Noah has been taken away from his parents!

B: You mean he was kidnapped?

A: No, by the police. **1.** He was undergoing chemo, but _____

_____.

B: Wasn't the chemo working?

A: **2.** It's too soon to know, but his mom said _____

_____.

B: That poor family. **3.** _____.

A: And poor Noah! A three-year-old shouldn't have to suffer like that.

1. 彼は化学療法を受けていたのですが，両親が代替療法を試すために彼をケンタッキーに連れて行ったのです。

2. まだ分からないのですが，母親によると彼はひどい気分変動を経験していました。

3. 彼らは息子のために最善を尽くしていました。

D Summary Practice: Fill in the blanks with suitable words beginning with the letters indicated.

◎ CD 25

A story coming out of (¹· **F**   ) raises the issue of
(²· **p**   ) (³· **r**   ). Three-year-old (⁴· **N**   )
McAdams was undergoing (⁵· **c**   )
after being diagnosed with (⁶· **l**   ). Claiming that the
treatment triggered violent (⁷· **m**   ) (⁸· **s**   ) in their son,
Noah's (⁹· **p**   ) took him out of state to try
(¹⁰· **a**   ) treatments. Although they maintained that
(¹¹· **t**   ) showed the (¹²· **c**   ) was gone, doctors in Florida
doubted the claim and had the boy taken from his home by the
(¹³· **p**   ). In what has become a legal (¹⁴· **t**   ) of (¹⁵· **w**   ), the
(¹⁶· **j**   ) has approved the parents' wish to try different treatments,
but ruled that they must undergo (¹⁷· **f**   ) more days of
chemo, and then be tested again. Noah's parents (¹⁸· **v**   ) to fight the
decision, citing their parental rights.

E Discussion: Share your ideas and opinions with your classmates.

1. This news story addresses the topic of parental rights. Look for other news stories related to this issue. Do you know of any similar cases here in Japan?

2. If you were the judge, how would you rule in this case? Discuss your ideas in a group.

Journey to the Edge

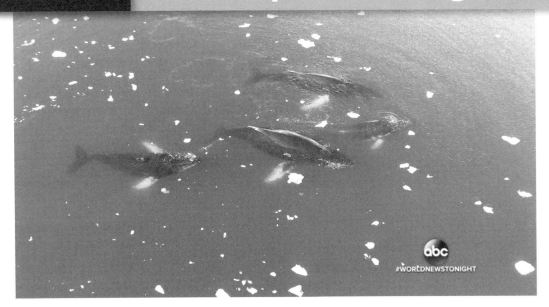

Before You Watch the News

Air Date: May 20, 2019
Duration: 2′ 11″

Preview Questions

1. What are scientists learning from humpback whales?
——ザトウクジラの調査で，科学者たちは何が分かりつつありますか。

2. How is the environment in the Antarctic Peninsula changing?
——南極半島では自然環境がどのように変化しつつありますか。

Warm-up Exercises

A Vocabulary Check: Choose the correct definition for each of the words below.

1. vital ( )

2. recede ( )

3. bedrock ( )

4. promote ( )

5. stunning ( )

a. base; solid foundation

b. extremely impressive or attractive

c. critical; very important

d. to move back; to pull back

e. to support; to further the progress of

B Fill in the blanks with appropriate expressions from the Vocabulary Check above. Change the word form where necessary.

1. Wow! That dress looks (   ) on you!
2. It's (   ) that you bring a copy of your passport when traveling overseas.
3. At Grandpa's funeral, he was praised for being the (   ) of the community.
4. Once the flood waters started to (   ), the clean-up activities began in full force.
5. One obvious way to (   ) diversity on campus is to actively recruit more international students.

News Story [2′ 11″]

D. Muir: An ABC News exclusive. Our journey to the bottom of the Earth tonight, where scientists are convinced that humpback whales can tell us a lot about climate change and its widespread effects. ABC's James Longman is in Antarctica as scientists take a major step tonight.   5

J. Longman: A journey to the ends of the Earth. Speeding across the frozen wilderness of Antarctica, we're tracking groups of humpback whales.   10
American scientists and the World Wildlife Fund here **1.** _____
_____ leading the search.

Scientist: We have sleeping whales up here. Can we get the tag pole ready?

J. Longman: We approach these awesome giants and get a view from above, gathering vital information to better understand the impact of climate   15
change.

So this is the whole point of this mission, to get as close as possible to these whales and tag them with these GPS systems that can tell us
2. _____ .

Across the Antarctic Peninsula, 87% of the glaciers here are receding, creating more open water, which has actually helped grow the humpback population. But warming waters are threatening a small crustacean called krill, the main food supply for humpbacks and the bedrock of

5

3. _____ .

A. Friedlaender, Institute of Marine Sciences, UC Santa Cruz: They represent   10
the health of an ocean ecosystem. To be able to have enough food to
support a whale, let alone a population of whales, **4.** _____
_____ to
promote life and to promote food being there.

J. Longman: After days of attempts to tag a whale, the scientists zero in. This   15
camera attached to the tracking device is successfully planted on the
humpback.

Brilliant!

5. _____
_____. Researchers finding plastics, heavy metals, even flame   20
retardants in their systems.

The science being pioneered here is some of the most important for the
survival of our planet. This place is stunning. But more than that, it can
tell us so much about the risks we all face. David?

D. Muir: All right, James Longman, our thanks to you and our team. And   25
James will have much more on those contaminants that **6.** _____
_____, plastics, those
heavy metals James mentioned. That's later tonight on *Nightline* on the
"Journey to the Edge."

Notes ABC News exclusive「ABC 放送独占ニュース」 bottom of the Earth「地球の底；南極」 humpback whales「ザトウクジラ」 take a major step「大きな一歩を踏み出す」 ends of the Earth「地球の果て；南極」 World Wildlife Fund「世界自然保護基金〈世界最大規模の自然環境保護団体で，国際的 NGO。気候変動，海洋保全など，持続可能な環境づくりがその活動の中心〉」 tag pole「タグポール〈クジラに GPS 追跡用の発信器を取り付けるためのポール〉」 tag them with ~「〜（無線発信器）を付ける」 Antarctic Peninsula「南極半島〈南極大陸から延びる細長い半島〉」 open water「開氷域；(開) 水面；(放) 水域〈島，岩礁，氷河のない水域で，クジラが自由に泳いだり，船舶が安全に航行が可能な水域のこと〉」 crustacean「甲殻類」 krill「オキアミ」 Institute of Marine Sciences「海洋科学研究所」 UC Santa Cruz「カリフォルニア大学サンタクルーズ校」 zero in「神経（注意力・努力）を集中する」 tracking device「追跡装置」 planted on ~「〜に埋め込んだ（取り付けた）」 heavy metals「重金属〈クジラには，重金属の一種であるメチル水銀が含まれることがある〉」 flame retardants「難燃剤〈プラスチックや繊維のような可燃素材を燃えにくくするために添加する化学物質〉」 systems「体内」 contaminants「汚染物質」 *Nightline*「ナイトライン〈ABC 放送による報道番組〉」

After You Watch the News

Exercises

A Listen to the CD and fill in the blanks in the text.　　　⊙ CD 26

B Multiple Choice Questions

1. Which is **NOT** a primary reason that scientists are in Antarctica?

   a. to observe the climate changes occurring there

   b. to learn about the sleeping habits of whales

   c. to better understand the impact of climate change worldwide

2. Humpback whales

   a. are decreasing in number.

   b. are moving away from Antarctica.

   c. are in danger of losing their main food source.

3. The scientists in Antarctica

   a. rely on drones to track the small crustaceans

   b. learn about the whales' behavior through GPS systems

   c. both *a* and *b*

4. Which of the following is **NOT** a likely consequence of the receding glaciers?

    a. the entire ecosystem will change

    b. the number of krill will dramatically decrease

    c. humpback whales will have to survive on plastics and heavy metals

C **Translate the following Japanese into English. Then listen to the CD and practice the conversation with your partner.** ⊙ CD 27

A: How was your trip to Antarctica?

B: That's a tough question to answer. ¹._____

_____.

A: Tell me the wonderful part first.

B: Well, the frozen wilderness is amazingly beautiful.

A: I could see that from your blog. And the terrible part?

B: ²._____,

   and we found that the krill are dying out.

A: Why is that such a big problem?

B: That's what the whales eat. ³._____

_____.

A: Gee, if I want to visit Antarctica, I'd better go now!

1. 素晴らしかったのと同時にひどかったです。

2. ひとつには，氷河が劇的に後退しつつあります。

3. 生態系全体が壊れそうなのです。

Summary Practice: Fill in the blanks with suitable words beginning with the letters indicated. ◎ CD 28

American Scientists and the (¹· **W**   ) (²· **W**   ) (³· **F**   ) have journeyed to the ends of the Earth to learn more about climate change. Their project focuses on observing the behavior of (⁴· **h**   ) whales in Antarctica, where (⁵· **e**   )-(⁶· **s**   ) percent of the (⁷· **g**   ) are receding. Using (⁸· **d**   ) and special (⁹· **t**   ) (¹⁰· **p**   ), the team attaches a GPS system to the animals to track their movement and (¹¹· **b**   ). They are making some alarming discoveries. Due to the shrinking ice, the whales actually have more open water, resulting in an (¹²· **i**   ) in the population. On the down side, their primary food source, the small (¹³· **c**   ) known as (¹⁴· **k**   ), are dying out as a result of the warmer water. The (¹⁵· **b**   ) of Antarctica's food chain, a decrease in the availability of krill will have dramatic effects on the entire (¹⁶· **e**   ) system. Add to this the presence of (¹⁷· **c**   ) like metals and flame (¹⁸· **r**   ) and it's obvious that scientists—and all of us— have a lot to worry about.

E **Discussion: Share your ideas and opinions with your classmates.**

1. How much do you know about Antarctica? Do an Internet search about some aspect of the region that interests you. Share your findings with the class.
2. Look for further information about either **humpback whales** OR **krill**.
3. The end of the news story focuses on contaminates found in the water. Is that a problem in Japan? Check about a local body of water and see what you can find out.

Air Date: March 28, 2019
Duration: 2′ 07″

Before You Watch the News

Preview Questions

1. Why was the funding for the Special Olympics at risk?
——スペシャル・オリンピックの予算がカットされそうになったのはなぜですか。

2. What did President Trump do about it?
——トランプ大統領はどのように対応しましたか。

Warm-up Exercises

A Vocabulary Check: Choose the correct definition for each of the words below.

1. override ( )
2. outrage ( )
3. skewer ( )
4. disabled ( )
5. authorize ( )

a. to give official permission; to approve

b. to overrule or reject

c. extreme shock or anger

d. to attack; to shower with questions (figurative use)

e. physically or mentally handicapped

B Fill in the blanks with appropriate expressions from the Vocabulary Check above. Change the word form where necessary.

1. The new chairman is expected to (   ) the committee's ban on hiring.

2. The whole town was in a state of (   ) when they learned of the mayor's scandalous actions.

3. That auditorium has excellent facilities for (   ) visitors.

4. If this latest misuse of funds is discovered, the coach will be (   ).

5. The department chair refused to (   ) the purchase of new AV equipment.

News Story [2′ 07″]

C. Vega: Battle over funding for the Special Olympics. Education Secretary Betsy DeVos taking heat on Capitol Hill again today for cutting the games from her budget. President Trump feeling the heat as well. And late today, a reversal, the president overriding the secretary, saying [1.] _____ _____. Here's ABC's senior congressional correspondent Mary Bruce.

M. Bruce: Facing growing outrage over his move to slash funding for the Special Olympics, tonight President Trump with an abrupt about-face.

President D. Trump: I've been to the Special Olympics. [2.] _____ _____.

M. Bruce: The administration called for cutting all federal money for the Special Olympics, $17.6 million. A tiny fraction of the president's $4.75 trillion budget. But a significant chunk of funding for the games, which give people with intellectual disabilities [3.] _____ _____. During two days of hearings on Capitol Hill, Trump's education secretary, Betsy DeVos, has been skewered.

Representative B. Lee: I still can't understand why you would go after disabled children in your budget. You zero that out! It's... it's appalling.

5

B. DeVos: Let me just...

Senator D. Durbin: Did you personally approve this... just... I think a yes or no will do. The $18 million cut of the funding for Special Olympics?

B. DeVos: No, 4. _____

_____.

10

Senator D. Durbin: Well, I wanna tell you, whoever came up with... whoever came up with that idea at OMB gets a special Olympic gold medal for insensitivity.

M. Bruce: Amid the outcry, Democrats and Republicans vowed not to authorize the cuts.

15

Representative K. McCarthy: No. I fully support, um, Special Olympics.

M. Bruce: Tonight the president claims it was all news to him and reversed course.

President D. Trump: 5. _____.

I have, ah, overridden my people. We're funding the Special Olympics.

20

C. Vega: OK, Mary Bruce joining us from Washington. Mary, President Trump overruling his own administration tonight. But it comes after lawmakers from both parties made it very clear they were not about to cut funding for the Special Olympics.

M. Bruce: Yeah, lawmakers were never going to give in to this request, but Secretary DeVos spent two days making the case for it anyway. And now tonight 6. _____, saying quote, "This is funding I have fought for behind the scenes for the last several years." Cecilia?

25

C. Vega: OK, Mary. Thank you.

30

Special Olympics「特別オリンピック；スペシャル・オリンピックス〈知的障がい者のためのオリンピック〉」 Education Secretary Betsy DeVos「ベッツィ・デヴォス教育長官」 taking heat on ~「〜において非難を浴びる」 Capitol Hill「連邦議会」 reversal「方針転換；逆転」 senior congressional correspondent「（連邦）議会担当主任記者」 slash「（予算を）大幅に削減する」 about-face「（方針の）完全な転換；180度の方針転換」 federal money「連邦予算」 tiny fraction「ごくわずか」 president's $4.75 trillion budget「4兆7千5百億ドルという大統領の政府予算（全体額）」 intellectual disabilities「知的障がい者」 hearings「公聴会；聴聞会」 Representative「下院議員」 go after ~「〜を狙う（〜を狙って予算を切り詰める）」 zero that out「（予算を）ゼロにする；取り除く」 appalling「ひどい；最低の；最悪の」 came up with ~「〜を考え出した；〜を思いついた；〜を発案した」 OMB「行政管理予算局（the Office of Management and Budget）〈アメリカ政府の行政機関の一つで，議会に送付する予算教書を作成し，成立した予算を執行することなどがその役割〉」 insensitivity「無神経さ；意識の希薄さ」 all news to ~「〜にとって初耳である；全く寝耳に水である」 my people「（政府）関係者」 lawmakers「（連邦議会）議員」 give in to ~「〜を受け入れる；〜に屈する」 making the case for ~「〜に対して賛成を主張する」

After ⟩ You Watch the News

Exercises

A Listen to the CD and fill in the blanks in the text.　　　　◎ CD 29

B Mark the following sentences true (T) or false (F) according to the information in the news story.

(　) **1.** The Special Olympics gives disabled people the chance to compete internationally.

(　) **2.** Funding for the Special Olympics is a significant chunk of the president's total budget.

(　) **3.** Both the education secretary and the president denied being involved in the decision to cut the funding.

(　) **4.** Senator Durbin wants to honor the person who had the idea to cut money for the games from the budget.

(　) **5.** Both Democrats and Republicans were strongly opposed to the cut.

(　) **6.** In the end, President Trump willingly overrode the request made by Betsy DeVos.

C Translate the following Japanese into English. Then listen to the CD and practice the conversation with your partner.   ⊙ CD 30

A: Are they really cutting funds for the next Special Olympics?

B: ¹· Betsy DeVos said so, but _____

_____.

A: I hope you're right. Do you remember my cousin's son? The disabled boy?

B: How could I forget little Stevie? He is such a lovable child!

A: He sure is. And tough, too! It turns out he's a great swimmer.

²·_____.

B: That would be fabulous! It's so exciting to watch them compete.

A: I couldn't agree with you more. ³· You can see the joy on their faces when

_____.

Hopefully, Stevie will have that chance, too.

1. ベッツィ・デヴォスは，そう言っていますが，トランプ大統領は絶対にそうさせないでしょう。

2. 彼は次のスペシャル・オリンピックスで，競技に出たいと願っています。

3. 世界の舞台で競技に出る機会が得られたなら，彼らの喜ぶ顔が見られることでしょう。

D Summary Practice: Fill in the blanks with suitable words beginning with the letters indicated.   ⊙ CD 31

The education secretary, (¹· **B**   ) (²· **D**   ), has spent a rough (³· **t**   ) days being skewered on (⁴· **C**   ) (⁵· **H**   ) over the recent decision to cut all of the (⁶· **f**   ) funding for the Special Olympics. The $(⁷· **e**   ) (⁸· **m**   ) earmarked for this event for (⁹· **d**   ) (¹⁰· **c**   ) is a small fraction of the Trump administration's total (¹¹· **b**   ) of over $(¹²· **f**   ) (¹³· **t**   ), and the proposed cut caused (¹⁴· **o**   ) among (¹⁵· **l**   ) from both parties. In the end, the president (¹⁶· **o**   ) the decision, adding that he thinks the Special Olympics are (¹⁷· **i**   ). For her part, DeVos claimed that she was not (¹⁸· **p**   ) involved in making the decision and that furthermore, she has been fighting for it (¹⁹· **b**   ) the (²⁰· **s**   ) for the last several years.

1. How much do you know about the Special Olympics? When did they start? Who started them? What sports are represented? Which countries compete? Use the Internet and see how much you can learn. Share your findings with the class.

2. The current education secretary, Betsy DeVos, has been a controversial figure for a number of reasons since being appointed by President Trump. See what you can find out about her background and her policies.

Pronunciation Hints from the News ②あいまい母音 /ə/ の発音

　たとえば about /əbaʊt/ の最初の母音 /ə/ は,「あいまい母音」(schwa) と呼ばれ, 英語の弱音節で一番よく現れる母音である。すべての母音の中で約 33% がこの音といわれている。日本語の「ア」の構えから少し口を閉じて, 唇は丸めずにあいまいに短く「ウ」と言うつもりで発音すると, この音になる。口の筋肉を緩めリラックスして発音するとよい。

　以下の例のように, behind の最初の音節はあいまい母音の /ə/ で発音されることが多いので「バァハインド」のように聞こえる。

— This is funding I have fought for ***behind*** the scenes ***for the*** last several years. *(Special Olympics Funding Furor, p.57)*

　以下の語にアクセントが置かれない場合は, あいまい母音で弱く発音されることが多い。

a /ə/, an /ən/, as /əz/, can /kən/, for /fɚ/, from /frəm/, has /həz/, the /ðə/, them /ðəm/, to /tə/, with /wəð/

— …Betsy DeVos taking heat on Capitol Hill again today ***for*** cutting ***the*** games from ***her*** budget. *(Special Olympics Funding Furor, p.56)*
— And late today, ***a*** reversal, ***the*** president overriding ***the*** secretary,… *(Special Olympics Funding Furor, p.56)*
— Facing growing outrage over his move ***to*** slash funding ***for the*** Special Olympics, tonight President Trump ***with an*** abrupt about-face. *(Special Olympics Funding Furor, p.56)*

News Story 11

American Heroes in Vietnam

 abc NEWS

Before You Watch the News

Air Date: February 28, 2019
Duration: 2′ 33″

Preview Questions

1. Why have some American veterans traveled to Vietnam?
——なぜアメリカの退役軍人がベトナムを訪れたのですか。

2. Who did they meet there?
——現地で誰と会いましたか。

Warm-up Exercises

A Vocabulary Check: Choose the correct definition for each of the words below.

1. pour （　）

2. eject （　）

3. sheer （　）

4. haunt （　）

5. polarizing （　）

a. to be forced or thrown out

b. to disturb; to preoccupy

c. to flow heavily

d. causing divisions or strong difference of opinion

e. absolute; complete

B Fill in the blanks with appropriate expressions from the Vocabulary Check above. Change the word form where necessary.

1. I got an A+ on my science test. It was (   ) luck!

2. We were worried when a brown liquid came (   ) out of the machine.

3. If you push this button on the toy, the rabbit (   ) from the car.

4. The senator's recent comments are so (   ).

5. The senior citizens who spoke to us were still (   ) by their memories of the bomb.

News Story [2′ 33″]

D. Muir: Finally, tonight here, the reunion here in Hanoi.

We have journeyed here before, to what's left of the prison known as the Hanoi Hilton. Where John McCain and so many other Americans were held prisoners of war. The rain pouring as we walked through. The prison cells, so little light. The bars on the windows.

1. _____

_____. John McCain was 31. An enemy missile would tear one of the wings off his bomber. He ejected. The sheer force of that moment breaking both of his arms and one of his legs.

Interviewer: What's your name?

J. McCain: Lieutenant Commander John McCain.

D. Muir: And in what's left of the prison now, we discover a book.

You can see here some of the American pilots who were arrested between 1964 and 1973.

The faces of the prisoners *2.* _____

And outside the Hanoi Hilton today, the men of Foxtrot 21. Marines who fought in Vietnam. Their battalion became known as the ghost battalion, because they lost so many. More than 50 years later, a reunion here in Vietnam, with help from the Greatest Generations Foundation. Lieutenant Colonel

James Page from Florida, who remembers Operation Harvest Moon, a battle that still haunts him.

Lieutenant Colonel J. Page: I lost 12 Marines that day. I was the company commander and ³. _____

_____. So I hope to go down and get peace when I go stand on the battlefield. I want to bury that.

D. Muir: Americans visit every day here. Remembering a polarizing time in America, and determined to remember those who served, too.

Tourist: We all lived so much of that, so to come here and um, almost, you know, ⁴. _____

_____ that we grew up with. It's important.

D. Muir: Joann Walker's husband served in Vietnam.

J. Walker: We talked more about it when we got here than we had ever. And it's emotional, because it was difficult, in a lot of ways.

D. Muir: And tonight, the veterans here ⁵. _____

_____ that was important to them on this trip. Getting the chance to meet some of the soldiers who they once fought against here in Vietnam. All of the men together, through shared pain. And tonight, through shared peace.

Veteran: It means a lot to us, it's closure for us. ⁶. _____

_____ and we got some great people here today and it just means a lot to us.

D. Muir: We thank them for their service and we thank them for sharing that moment with us today. I'm David Muir. I hope to see you right back here tomorrow night. Good night.

Notes   **what's left of ~**「～の（建物が）残っている」   **Hanoi Hilton**「ハノイ・ヒルトン〈ホアロー捕虜収容所（Hoa Lo Prison）の別称。ベトナム戦争で捕虜となったアメリカ軍兵士を収容した捕虜収容所〉」 **John McCain**「ジョン・マケイン（元上院議員）〈1936-2018年。ベトナム戦争当時は戦闘機のパイロットだった。撃墜され脱出後に捕虜として捕まりハノイ・ヒルトンで5年半過ごした〉」 **prisoners of war**「戦争捕虜」 **bomber**「爆撃機」 **Lieutenant Commander**「少佐」 **Foxtrot 21**「フォックストロット21大隊」 **battalion**「大隊（海兵隊）」 **Greatest Generations Foundation**「グレイテスト・ジェネレーション財団〈退役軍人を支援するアメリカの非政府組織（NGO）〉」 **Lieutenant Colonel**「中佐」 **Operation Harvest Moon**「ハーベスト・ムーン作戦〈アメリカ海兵隊が1965年12月にベトコンとの間に展開した戦闘作戦〉」 **company commander**「中隊長；中隊の司令官」 **go down**「（ベトナム）に来る」 **lived so much of that**「（ベトナム戦争当時は）たくさんつらい事を経験してきた。(*We feel like*) we all lived *through* so much of that. *through* が抜けている」 **closure**「（気持ちの）区切り」

Background of the News

　ベトナム戦争は，もともと南北に分かれていたベトナムで起きた内戦である。南ベトナムを支援して介入したアメリカは，北ベトナムの共産党政権が南に及ぶことを強く警戒し，1965年の2月に北ベトナムに空爆（北爆）を開始したため，ベトナム戦争は全面的な戦争に突入した。しかし，アメリカ軍は南ベトナム解放民族戦線（ベトコン）のゲリラ戦術に苦しめられ，1973年の和平協定でアメリカ軍は撤退することになった。1975年4月には南ベトナム政府は無条件降伏し，ベトナムは北ベトナムによって統一され，翌年には現在のベトナム社会主義共和国が成立した。

　本ニュースストーリーで紹介されているハノイのホアロー収容所（Hoa Lo Prison）は，フランス統治時代の19世紀末に独立運動家を収容する監獄として建てられ，ベトナム戦争では北ベトナム軍の米兵捕虜収容施設として使われた。米兵捕虜からは皮肉を込めてハノイ・ヒルトン（Hanoi Hilton）と呼ばれていた。

　読売新聞（2018/09/23）によると，ジョン・マケイン（John McCain）氏は海軍パイロットとしてベトナム戦争に従軍し，1967年10月，ハノイ上空で撃墜されて捕虜となった。父親が米軍幹部だったため，当時の北ベトナム当局は早期解放をもちかけたが，本人は捕虜全員の解放を求めて拒否した。戦争終結まで5年半にわたり拷問を伴う過酷な監禁生活を送った後，「ベトナム戦争の英雄」として米国に帰還し，40代半ばでアリゾナ州から連邦議員に選出された。また，2008年の大統領選では共和党候補として，民主党のオバマ前大統領と争ったが2018年8月に亡くなった。

After   You Watch the News

Exercises

A Listen to the CD and fill in the blanks in the text.   ◎ CD 32

B Multiple Choice Questions

1. The marines of Foxtrot 21
   a. killed more enemy soldiers than any other battalion.
   b. returned to Vietnam for the first time in over 50 years.
   c. were haunted by ghosts while they were fighting in Vietnam.

2. What *DIDN'T* the war veterans do in Vietnam during their recent visit?
   a. meet some of their former enemies
   b. meet Lieutenant Commander John McCain
   c. visit the place where some American soldiers were imprisoned

3. Lieutenant Colonel Page wants to go to the battlefield
   a. to bury some of the soldiers who died there.
   b. to look for some of the Marines who were lost.
   c. to make peace in his mind over what happened there.

4. The Hanoi Hilton
   a. has recently been converted from a prison to a hotel.
   b. has become a popular destination for American tourists.
   c. remains open with help from the Greatest Generations Fund.

C Translate the following Japanese into English. Then listen to the CD and practice the conversation with your partner.

CD 33

A: Mom, how was the trip to Hanoi? Was Dad okay?

B: It was very emotional for him, but I think he finally found closure.

A: ¹._____.

B: He did while we were there. He talked a lot about the other Marines in the ghost battalion when we visited the Hanoi Hilton.

A: ²._____?

B: He did! ³. And amazingly,_____

_____, too.

A: Wow! Shared pain and shared peace. How wonderful for all of them.

1. そこで経験したことについてほとんど何も話しません。
2. 実際そこで昔の友達と会ったのですか。
3. そして驚いたことに，ベトナム人兵士たちと新しい友達ができました。

CD 34

Former U.S. (¹· **M**   ) traveled from across the U.S. to
(²· **H**   ) for a (³· **r**   ) that included a visit to the
infamous Hanoi Hilton, where John McCain and many other Americans
were once held as (⁴· **p**   ) of war. In what remains of the
dark prison with its concrete walls and (⁵· **n**   ) beds, they
discovered a (⁶· **b**   ) with photos of some of the American
(⁷· **p**   ) who were forced to stay there in the 1960s and 1970s. With
the assistance of the (⁸· **G**   ) (⁹· **G**   )
Foundation, some of the Marines from Foxtrot 21, known as the
(¹⁰· **g**   ) (¹¹· **b**   ), came to find (¹²· **c**   )
from battlefield losses that haunt them to this day. It was an
(¹³· **e**   ) trip, all the more so since the former Marines had
the chance to meet Vietnamese soldiers who were once their
(¹⁴· **e**   ). It was a meaningful (¹⁵· **j**   ) for all.

E Discussion: Share your ideas and opinions with your classmates.

1. The war in Vietnam was a difficult time for the United States. Do an
Internet search to see what you can learn about this complex war. How
did the war begin and end? Which countries were involved?

2. A number of popular movies were made about the war in Vietnam,
including *The Deer Hunter* (1978), *Platoon* (1986), *Good Morning,
Vietnam* (1987) and *Born on the Fourth of July* (1989). If you have a
chance, try to watch one of them. How is the war in Vietnam depicted?

3. If you have an elderly relative who lived through World War II in Japan,
talk to him or her about their experiences. Share the information with
your classmates.

Measles Outbreak Quarantine in L.A.

Before You Watch the News

Air Date: April 25, 2019
Duration: 2' 26"

Preview Questions

1. How widespread is the current outbreak of measles in the U.S.?
   ——アメリカで，はしかの流行はどのような状態ですか。

2. What measures are being taken to contain it?
   ——伝染を防ぐためにどのような方策がとられていますか。

Warm-up Exercises

A Vocabulary Check: Choose the correct definition for each of the words below.

1. expose （　）　　　　**a.** huge

2. access （　）　　　　**b.** to reveal; to uncover

3. massive （　）　　　　**c.** to stay in a place longer than necessary

4. exquisitely （　）　　**d.** a way in; a means of entry

5. linger （　）　　　　**e.** extremely; perfectly

B Fill in the blanks with appropriate expressions from the Vocabulary Check above. Change the word form where necessary.

1. Don't (   ) in the hallway! Some students are still taking exams.
2. The latest investigation (   ) a drug ring that included several foreigners.
3. Jeff accumulated (   ) debt after buying a sports car and a yacht.
4. My engagement ring has an (   ) formed diamond in the shape of a heart.
5. Sam will be spending his vacation in a mountain village with no Internet (   ).

News Story [2' 26"]

T. Llamas: Breaking news in the measles outbreak, spreading across this country. The worst in 25 years. And tonight, hundreds of students and faculty at two major universities in Los Angeles are under quarantine.

5

After the illness was nearly eradicated, ¹·_____ _____. Look at the map right there.

How are these latest cases at the universities exposed? ABC's chief national correspondent Matt Gutman starts us off in L.A.

10

M. Gutman: Tonight, that measles scare racing through two of the biggest university systems in the country. Many dozens possibly exposed to what is considered ²·_____ _____.

15

Dr. M. Davis, Los Angeles County Health Department: We have five cases, uh, um, four of which are linked as an outbreak um, that stemmed from a traveler who was unvaccinated.

M. Gutman: That traveler, coming in from abroad, apparently going through Los Angeles Airport, ³·_____

20

_____, on April 1st, and then going on to UCLA with its 45,000 students to the psychology department on three days in early April.

Dr. M. Davis: A few of the cases have been in other places, attending, you know, UCLA classes, as well as being at Cal State LA in the library. And as a result of that, **4.** _____ _____, uh, that may have been exposed.

M. Gutman: That Cal State library, one of the most visited spots on campus.

Health official: Two thousand visitors in that library a day, most of them don't sign in or out. So, we've had a lot of exposure to folks that we actually can't identify.

M. Gutman: Over 300 students and faculty now under quarantine at the two universities **5.** _____ _____.

Dr. M. Davis: If they are not immune to measles, then they must be kept away from others in order to not have that unintentional spread of measles should they come in contact with others who may not be as immune as well.

T. Llamas: And Matt Gutman joins us now live. Matt, **6.** _____ _____? And what does it mean for all these people, because this is a massive amount of people right now?

M. Gutman: Measles is an exquisitely contagious virus. It can linger in the air for two hours, sometimes more. Its incubation period, Tom, is 21 days. Now, some of those students and faculty will be able to quickly produce their medical records, likely those younger students. But **7.** _____ _____ may have a harder time finding them and they could stay in quarantine for up to two more weeks. Tom?

T. Llamas: Matt Gutman with that breaking news tonight. Matt, thank you.

Notes **breaking news**「ニュース速報；最新ニュース」 **measles outbreak**「はしかの大流行（感染拡大；発生）」 **faculty**「教職員；大学教員」 **under quarantine**「検疫下に置かれて；隔離されて；（はしかの伝染を予防するために）検疫する」 **eradicated**「根絶される」 **chief national correspondent**「国内担当主任記者」 **starts us off in ~**「～から（ニュースを）伝える」 **university systems**「大学群；（カリフォルニア州が設置する総合州立）大学システム〈University system とは，複数の州立大学によって構成されるエリア別の大学群のこと〉」 **Many dozens**「何十人もの；たくさんの」 **County Health Department**「郡保健（衛生）局」 **stemmed from ~**「～に由来する；～が原因の」 **unvaccinated**「ワクチン接種歴のない；予防接種を受けていない」 **Cal State LA**「カリフォルニア州立大学ロサンゼルス校 =California State University, Los Angeles(CSULA)〈約2万人以上の学生が学んでいる州立総合大学で，カリフォルニア州全土に 23 のキャンパスを持つ米国最大級の大学群であるカリフォルニア州立大学（California State University）のひとつ〉」 **sign in or out**「入館・退館の記録を残す」 **immune to ~**「～に対して免疫がある」 **incubation period**「潜伏期間」

Background of the News

　世界で，はしかが広まっている。WHO によると，2019年1～3月の世界の感染者は約11万2千人で，前年同期の約4倍になり，感染報告は発展途上国を中心に 170 カ国にのぼっている。アメリカではニューヨーク市が 2019年4月，ブルックリン地区の一部に「公衆衛生上の非常事態」を宣言した。アメリカでは，宗教上の理由でワクチン接種を避けたり，「ワクチンは危険だ」とするニセ情報が SNS で拡散されたりして，それを信じた親が子どもにワクチンを接種させないため，はしかの免疫を持たない（not immune to measles）子どもが増えているという。

　日本でもはしかの感染拡大（measles outbreak）が続いている。産経新聞（2019/05/05）は，2019年4月14日までの累積患者数が 28 都道府県で 406 人にのぼり，都道府県別で最も多いのは大阪の 131 人であると，国立感染症研究所の発表を引用している。日本はワクチン接種の普及により，感染を防ぐ免疫保有率が 95％を超えており，世界保健機関（WHO）は 2015年，日本をウイルスによる感染がないはしかの「排除状態」と認定していた。

After　You Watch the News

Exercises

A Listen to the CD and fill in the blanks in the text.　　　　　◎ CD 35

B Multiple Choice Questions

1. The current measles outbreak
   a. has so far only affected students.
   b. is expected to be over in a few days.
   c. has largely been the result of unintentional contact.

2. The measles virus
   a. has a longer incubation period than it used to.
   b. had nearly disappeared but has now come back.
   c. is believed to be less contagious than it used to be.

3. The group now in quarantine
   a. had all recently traveled.
   b. includes some people who were vaccinated and others who were not.
   c. is not being allowed to leave their dormitory rooms.

4. Which of the following recently occurred at UCLA?
   a. The measles started in the psychology department.
   b. Over 300 students and faculty were quarantined.
   c. An unvaccinated traveler brought the measles virus to the library.

C Translate the following Japanese into English. Then listen to the CD and practice the conversation with your partner. ◎ CD 36

A: I haven't seen Becky all week. What's she up to?
B: Haven't you heard? **1.**_____.
A: How did that happen?
B: She's been spending a lot of time in the Cal State library. She thinks she may have been exposed to the measles.
A: **2.** _____?
   Most people our age were.
B: She's trying to find out, but her parents are traveling right now.
A: **3.** Well,_____.

1. 彼女は検疫を受けています。
2. 子どもの頃，ワクチン接種をしなかったのですか。
3. さて，もし免疫がないのなら，あとで後悔するよりも，用心に越したことはありません。

D Summary Practice: Fill in the blanks with suitable words beginning with the letters indicated.

⊙ CD 37

One of the world's most (¹· **c**   ) viruses, the measles, is in the news due to an (²· **o**   ) that has already spread to (³· **t**   )-(⁴· **t**   ) states. Thought to have been almost entirely (⁵· **e**   ), this outbreak is the worst in (⁶· **t**   )-(⁷· **f**   ) years. Two (⁸· **u**   ) in the (⁹· **L**   ) (¹⁰· **A**   ) area are trying to keep the measles from spreading on their campuses after (¹¹· **f**   ) cases were confirmed, four believed to have been infected by an (¹²· **u**   ) traveler. That traveler arrived at Los Angeles (¹³· **A**   ) from (¹⁴· **a**   ) on April 1, then spent three days in the UCLA (¹⁵· **p**   ) (¹⁶· **d**   ). Other people may have been exposed at the Cal State LA (¹⁷· **l**   ). Over 300 (¹⁸· **f**   ) and (¹⁹· **s**   ) are now in (²⁰· **q**   ) while they confirm from their (²¹· **m**   ) records whether or not they are (²²· **i**   ). With an (²³· **i**   ) period of (²⁴· **t**   )-(²⁵· **o**   ) days, they have to be certain in order not to unintentionally spread the virus to others. During that time, they will have no (²⁶· **a**   ) to (²⁷· **p**   ) areas or dorms.

E Discussion: Share your ideas and opinions with your classmates.

1. Look for stories about students being quarantined in Japan. (Hint: in recent years there have been quarantines for contagious diseases like bird flu and swine flu.) What are some of the concerns when students are not allowed to attend classes?

2. Vaccinations for measles and certain other childhood diseases are controversial. See what you can find out about this issue. Were you vaccinated for measles as a child?

Useful Grammar from the News ③客観性を示す表現

　ニュース報道内容の客観性，中立性を示すため，特に未確認情報の場合は allegedly（伝えられるところでは）apparently, possibly（おそらくは）など，断定を避けるための副詞が使われる。

— That traveler, coming in from abroad, **apparently** going through
　Los Angeles Airport,... *(Measles Outbreak Quarantine in L.A., p.68)*

　上記の例では，「外国からやってきた旅行者が，**おそらく**ロサンゼルス空港から…」というように断定を避けた表現が使われている。

— Many dozens **possibly** exposed to what is considered...
(Measles Outbreak Quarantine in L.A., p.68)

— The actress who played a role model on *Full House* **allegedly**
　shelling out $500,000 to consultant Rick Singer,...
(College Scandal Shock Waves, p.90)

　他にも，形容詞の alleged や it is believed のような表現も断定を避けるために使われる。

— Fellow or former students, **it's believed**, who rushed the schools
　and opened fire. *(Columbine: 20 Years Later, p.83)*
— ...after being arrested today for her **alleged** role in that sweeping
　college bribery scheme. *(College Scandal Shock Waves, p.89)*
— ..., the students, were unaware, but **it's believed** some might have
　known. *(College Scandal Shock Waves, p.91)*

Mayors Challenge Trump

Air Date: April 13, 2019
Duration: 2′ 13″

Preview Questions

1. What has President Trump suggested doing with some undocumented immigrants?

——不法移民に対応するために，どのような方策をとると大統領は提案していますか。

2. How are some U.S. mayors reacting?

——アメリカの市長たちは，どのような反応を示していますか。

Warm-up Exercises

A Vocabulary Check: Choose the correct definition for each of the words below.

1. outrageous ( )

2. float ( )

3. contradict ( )

4. apprehend ( )

5. federal ( )

a. to oppose; to challenge

b. to arrest; to capture

c. to propose; to suggest

d. national

e. shocking; shameful

B Fill in the blanks with appropriate expressions from the Vocabulary Check above. Change the word form where necessary.

1. The thief was (   ) within an hour of stealing the car.
2. How could anyone wear such a tiny bikini in public? It's (   )!
3. We'll need to apply for (   ) funds if we want to repair those bridges.
4. If the idea of a dress code is (   ), a lot of people will be upset.
5. Don't (   ) me in front of the children!

News Story [2′ 13″]

T. Llamas: Politics now and the increasing tensions between the president and his political foes over developments at the border.

1. _____
_____

heading for the U.S. continuing to frustrate President Trump. The president pushing an idea to release undocumented immigrants into so-called sanctuary cities, catching some on his own team off guard.

But some big city leaders are now welcoming the idea. ABC White House   10
correspondent Tara Palmeri with more.

T. Palmeri: Tonight, 2. _____ are challenging President Trump's latest proposal to transport migrants from detention centers along the southern border to so-called sanctuary cities. From Oakland...   15

Mayor L. Schaaf, Oakland, California: This is an outrageous abuse of power and public resources.

T. Palmeri: ...to Seattle...

Mayor J. Durkan, Seattle, Washington: 3. _____
_____ will stand up against a president who divides   20
America.

T. Palmeri: ...to San Jose.

Mayor S. Liccardo, San Jose, California:
   The threats of the president
   certainly don't amount to threats
   to us.

T. Palmeri: The city's leaders, including
   Chicago's incoming mayor Lori Lightfoot, saying they will welcome
   migrants.

Mayor-elect L. Lightfoot, Chicago, Illinois: And we're gonna do everything we
   can to make sure that **4.** _____   10
   _____, whatever their immigration status is, are gonna be treated fairly
   and with respect.

T. Palmeri: Just 24 hours ago, the White House saying the idea to bus migrants
   was floated and rejected. It was dismissed by the Department of
   Homeland Security, but the president quickly contradicted his own   15
   administration.

President D. Trump: We are looking at the possibility, strongly looking at it,
   5. _____.

T. Palmeri: Tonight a White House spokesperson telling ABC News they are
   taking the proposal seriously and they've launched a review on how it   20
   would work and how much it would cost. It's the latest sign of the
   president's growing frustration with what he calls **6.** _____
   _____.

   Last month, 103,000 migrants were either apprehended or stopped at the
   border, the highest number in over a decade.   25

President D. Trump: They're coming like it's a picnic, because, let's go to
   Disneyland.

T. Palmeri: **7.** _____ transporting
   migrants to one of these locations. There are more than 30, called
   sanctuary cities, because they choose not to follow federal immigration   30
   laws.

President D. Trump: They want more people in their sanctuary cities, well, we'll give them more people. We can give them a lot. We can give them an unlimited supply. And ^{8.} _____ _____. They say, "We have open arms." They're always saying they have open arms. Let's see if they have open arms.

Notes   **developments at the border**「国境での (不法移民問題の) 展開」 **undocumented immigrants**「不法移民」 **sanctuary cities**「サンクチュアリー・シティ；聖域都市 〈不法移民に寛容な郡や市の通称で, 不法移民の強制送還を求める入国管理当局への協力を拒否している。聖域都市は民主党が優勢なサンフランシスコ, ロサンゼルス, ニューヨークなどの大都市部に多く, 全米各地に 30 都市以上にのぼる〉」 **catching ~ off guard**「(予期せぬ大統領の発言が) ~を驚かせた」 **White House correspondent**「ホワイトハウス担当記者」 **detention centers**「(移民) 拘留所 (センター)；収容施設」 **Oakland**「オークランド 〈カリフォルニア州西部, サンフランシスコ湾に臨む港市〉」 **public resources**「公的資源 (資金) 〈聖域都市に不法移民をバスで輸送するのにかかる費用〉」 **Seattle**「シアトル 〈ワシントン州西部に位置し, 同州最大の都市。不法移民の居住者も多い〉」 **stand up against ~**「~に立ち向かう；~に異を唱える；~に抵抗する」 **San Jose**「サンホゼ 〈カリフォルニア州西部の都市で, サンフランシスコ南方に位置する〉」 **threats of the president**「大統領からの脅し (圧力) 〈聖域都市に対して, 連邦政府による州への補助金を減額するなどの脅しを行ってきた〉」 **amount to ~**「~を意味する；~に等しい」 **incoming mayor**「後任新市長 〈現職のラーム・エマニュエル市長の後任としてライトフット氏は 2019 年 5 月, アフリカ系米国人女性として初めてのシカゴ市長となった〉」 **immigration status**「入国 (在留) 資格 〈居住者が正規の在留資格を有しているか, あるいは不法移民かの区別〉」 **dismissed**「却下された；棄却された」 **Department of Homeland Security**「国土安全保障省 〈2001 年 9 月 11 日に発生した同時多発テロの教訓に基づき設立された〉」 **strongly looking at it**「(聖域都市への不法移民移送案を) 真剣に検討している」 **spokesperson**「報道官」 **frustration**「不満 〈大統領選で移民対策を主要テーマに掲げていたトランプ大統領は, 民主党が移民法改正に後ろ向きのため, 不法移民対策が進まないことに業を煮やしている〉」 **They're coming like it's a picnic, because, let's go to Disneyland.**「〈It's appealing and attracting a large number of people like a picnic or Disneyland. という主旨のことをのべている〉」 **immigration laws**「(連邦) 移民法 〈アメリカに滞在する権利のない不法移民を退去させるための法律〉」

Background of the News

　強硬な不法移民対策を公約に掲げるトランプ大統領は，不法移民（undocumented immigrants）の摘発に着手している。産経新聞（2019/07/17）によると，不法移民のうち，裁判所から退去命令を受けたにもかかわらず，アメリカ国内にとどまっている約 2,000 世帯が対象で，ニューヨーク，シカゴ，サンフランシスコなどで行われ，拘束後は母国に送還するという。これに対して，ニューヨークやシカゴなど不法移民に寛容な聖域都市（sanctuary city）と呼ばれる自治体や移民団体は強く反発しており，各地で抗議デモが行われた。聖域都市では，不法移民を保護し，連邦政府の不法移民取り締まりに協力せず，住民の滞在資格を問わないなどの措置を取ることで彼らと共存しようとしている。

　トランプ大統領は，メキシコとの国境沿いの収容施設（detention center）で，収容能力を超える不法移民が拘束されている問題で，聖域都市に移民を解放（release）することを「まじめに検討している」と語った。トランプ大統領は，聖域都市に対して「（不法移民の）無制限の供給（unlimited supply）が可能だ」と述べた。これは，強硬な不法移民取り締まりに抵抗する民主党を牽制する意図があるものとみられる。

After　You Watch the News

Exercises

A Listen to the CD and fill in the blanks in the text.　 CD 38

B Multiple Choice Questions

1. The news story suggests that President Trump's frustration is mostly due to
    a. an increasing number of sanctuary cities near the border.
    b. an increasing number of migrants trying to enter the United States.
    c. some mayors and his own administration disagreeing with his ideas.

2. Who has disagreed with the president?
    a. the mayors of some sanctuary cities
    b. the Department of Homeland Security
    c. both *a* and *b*

3. According to the president, sanctuary cities

    a. are dividing the country.

    b. tend not to follow the national laws.

    c. are offering free food and entertainment to new migrants.

4. Which of the following statements is **NOT** true?

    a. The mayors quoted in the news story do not feel threatened by the president.

    b. The leaders of some sanctuary cities claim that they would be pleased to welcome more migrants.

    c. There is a plan to bus undocumented migrants away from detention centers because they are being abused.

C **Translate the following Japanese into English. Then listen to the CD and practice the conversation with your partner.**　◎ CD 39

A: Your son's family is living in Seattle now, aren't they?

B: That's right. ¹·_____. They love it!

A: ²·_____?

B: Don't be silly! Seattle welcomes immigrants. That diversity is one of the reasons they enjoy living there so much.

A: But President Trump just announced he's gonna bus undocumented immigrants to those places. Doesn't that concern you?

B: ³·_____

_____. If it does happen, though, they'll be better off in Seattle than in those detention centers.

A: We'll just have to wait and see what happens, I guess.

1. そこで５年近く暮らしています。

2. 彼らが聖域都市に住んでいることで不安はないのですか。

3. 彼の言うことを真剣にとらえてよいか，全く分かりません。

Summary Practice: Fill in the blanks with suitable words beginning with the letters indicated.   ⊙ CD 40

The nightly news shows continue to show images of large numbers of
(¹· **m**   ) heading to the U.S. (²· **b**   ), causing
President Trump to feel increasingly (³· **f**   ). In a move
that surprised some members of his own (⁴· **t**   ) and was in fact
rejected by the Department of (⁵· **H**   ) (⁶· **S**   ),
the president has proposed a new idea that some are calling
(⁷· **o**   ): to bus (⁸· **u**   )
(⁹· **i**   ) to (¹⁰· **s**   ) cities around the
U.S. With over 100,000 migrants arriving at the border last month alone,
the highest figure in more than a (¹¹· **d**   ), the proposed program,
if actually carried out, could involve huge numbers of people. The
(¹²· **m**   ) of some of the sanctuary cities, including
(¹³· **S**   ) and (¹⁴· **C**   ), are challenging the president,
even saying that they would welcome new arrivals from the
(¹⁵· **d**   ) centers. Will the (¹⁶· **W**   ) (¹⁷· **H**   )
follow through with the president's plan? We'll have to wait and see.

E **Discussion: Share your ideas and opinions with your classmates.**

1. Immigration at the southern U.S. border is a huge and complex issue. Where do the immigrants come from? Why are they trying to enter the U.S.? Why has the number of immigrants increased so dramatically?

2. Do an Internet search on sanctuary cities. What do you think of the idea?

3. The U.S. is a country of immigrants. See if you can find the country of origin of these famous Americans:

Albert Einstein Arnold Schwarzenegger Melania Trump
John Lennon Madeleine Albright

News Story 14

Columbine: 20 Years Later

Before You Watch the News

Air Date: April 20, 2019
Duration: 2′ 38″

Preview Questions

1. What happened at Columbine High School 20 years ago today?
   ——20 年前の今日，コロンバイン高校では何が起こりましたか。

2. What changes have taken place since that time?
   ——この事件以来，変化したことは何ですか。

Warm-up Exercises

A Vocabulary Check: Choose the correct definition for each of the words below.

1. grim (　)
2. etch (　)
3. infatuation (　)
4. confront (　)
5. resiliency (　)

a. passion; obsession

b. to engrave or carve, literally or figuratively

c. strength; resistance

d. depressing; gloomy

e. to challenge or defy

B Fill in the blanks with appropriate expressions from the Vocabulary Check above. Change the word form where necessary.

1. If you think their plan is stupid, you'd better (   ) them before it's too late.

2. My sister has seen that movie six times already! She has a real (   ) for the main actor.

3. Living abroad is exciting, but it requires a great deal of (   ).

4. Chris has looked so (   ) since his friends moved to California.

5. Tom wants to have his fiancée's name (   ) on his wedding band.

News Story [2′ 38″]

T. Llamas: Next to the grim anniversary back here at home. Twenty years ago today, the Columbine High School massacre.

Memories seared in the nation's mind of teenagers **1.** _____

_____, barely escaping after two seniors launched a violent planned attack, killing 12 students and a teacher. A number of memorials and vigils this weekend. Many of the survivors now with children of their own. Here's ABC's Clayton Sandell.

C. Sandell: Tonight, remembering the 12 students and one teacher **2.** _____ at Columbine High.

City official 1: On April 20, 1999, the forces of evil did not win.

City official 2: Darkness cannot win. Evil never has the last word. Death does not have the last word.

C. Sandell: The day etched in history when **3.** _____

_____, a horror playing out on live TV.

P. Jennings, ABC News: Fellow or former students, it's believed, who rushed the schools and opened fire.

C. Sandell: Columbine was not the first school shooting, but it marked a violent new era of deadly tragedy. Virginia Tech, Sandy Hook, Parkland and others. An ABC News investigation found Columbine may have inspired **4.** _____ _____, plots or threats. Just this week, police say an 18-year-old Florida high school senior who bought a shotgun, forcing more than 100 Colorado schools to shut down, had a Columbine infatuation.

In 1999, Sean Graves was shot six times.

S. Graves, shot at Columbine: I need to, uh, do more physical therapy before I'll know if I'll walk.

C. Sandell: Now he fears for his own kids.

S. Graves: Now that I'm a parent, **5.** _____ _____ 24 hours a day, seven days a week, 3-6-5.

C. Sandell: At Columbine, police were criticized for not moving in faster. Today, officers are trained to confront shooters immediately.

Police officer: Suspect down.

A. Lemus-Paiz, Columbine High School senior: The first day of class of a new school year, of a new semester, I'll walk in and I'll be like, okay, like, **6.** _____? Like, where's the best place to hide, like, if something happens?

C. Sandell: The day also forever changing the way kids, parents and schools think about safety.

T. Llamas: No doubt a dark turning point for our country, and Clayton, so powerful to hear from those survivors 20 years later and we know that at

5

10

15

20

25

30

the high school, the survivors and the students have tried to make this day 7. _____.

C. Sandell: That's right, Tom. They call it a day of service.

We saw hundreds of students, teachers and faculty picking up rakes and shovels, taking on dozens of community projects all to do a little bit of good and 8. _____, the current principal here at Columbine told a memorial service crowd that Columbine is not only a model of resiliency, it is thriving.

5

After You Watch the News

Exercises

A Listen to the CD and fill in the blanks in the text.

⦿ CD 41

B Multiple Choice Questions

1. The Columbine massacre
   a. was the first high school shooting in the U.S.
   b. inspired deadly attacks in hundreds of schools.
   c. resulted in 13 deaths and marked a new era of violence.

2. As a result of the Columbine shooting
   a. Columbine is no longer known as a model of resiliency.
   b. police officers are trained about confronting shooters.
   c. students are taught about hiding places on the first day of school.

3. The massacre at Columbine High School
   a. was inspired by an earlier school shooting.
   b. was carried out by two Columbine students.
   c. caused 100 other Colorado schools to close down.

4. Which did *NOT* happen on the 20th anniversary of the shooting?
   a. Memorial services were held.
   b. Columbine students, faculty and staff performed community service.
   c. Survivors and current Columbine students remained inside the school to focus on the tragedy.

C Translate the following Japanese into English. Then listen to the CD and practice the conversation with your partner. CD 42

A: Can it really be that 20 years have passed since that awful day?
B: It's unbelievable. **1.**_____.
A: And what's changed? Just this week a student in Florida bought a shotgun.
B: Yeah. They said that student had an infatuation with the Columbine massacre.
A: **2.** And now _____.
B: Speaking of kids, it looks like yours are waiting for you to join in the clean-up activities.
A: You're right. **3.** _____. Let's go!

1. 私たちの高校はあの悲劇のために有名になってしまいました。
2. そして今は，私たちの子どもたちの安全を心配しないといけません。
3. 今日は暗い話はもうたくさんです。

D Summary Practice: Fill in the blanks with suitable words beginning with the letters indicated.

CD 43

On the (¹· t   ) anniversary of the (²· m   ) at Columbine High School, people across America are remembering the scenes of students with their (³· h   ) up, escaping from the (⁴· v   ) attack. Many of those students are now (⁵· p   ) themselves, concerned with (⁶· p   ) their own children. The Columbine massacre continues to (⁷· i   ) similar haunting incidents like those at Virginia Tech, (⁸· S   ) (⁹· H   ) and (¹⁰· P   ), among others. More recently, an 18-year-old (¹¹· s   ) in (¹²· F   ) with a (¹³· s   ) and a Columbine (¹⁴· i   ) was arrested. When will it end? To show their (¹⁵· r   ), the Columbine community decided to mark the anniversary with a day of (¹⁶· s   ). In addition to the memorial services and (¹⁷· v   ), hundreds of students and teachers engaged in local projects to prove that (¹⁸· d   ) cannot win.

E Discussion: Share your ideas and opinions with your classmates.

1. Violence in American schools has been a big topic for many years. Why do you think school violence is so prevalent in the U.S.? Do an Internet search for information on gun ownership laws in the U.S.
2. Four different school shootings are mentioned in this ABC News story. Choose one of them and see what you can find out about the shooters, the victims, and any changes that may have been brought about as a result of that shooting.

Pronunciation Hints from the News ③カタカナ英語発音

下記の例では，model /mɑdl/ は 2 音節語で「マドゥ」のように聞こえる。しかし，いわゆるカタカナ英語的に発音すると「モデル」となり，語尾に余分な母音の「ウ」が入ってしまう。

— …Columbine is not only a *model* of resiliency, it is thriving.

(Columbine: 20 Years Later, p.84)

日本語の音の単位はモーラ（拍）（mora）と呼ばれ，基本的に仮名 1 文字に相当する。たとえば，「クルマ」は 3 モーラで，/ku-ru-ma/ のように子音と母音とが交互にくる。英語の street/striːt/ は 1 音節だが，モーラ単位の日本語の音韻体系で発音すると「ス・ト・リ・ー・ト」のようになり 5 モーラになる。日本人が英語を発音する際，どうしてもカタカナ英語発音になりがちなのは，日本語のモーラに影響されるからである。以下の例でも「ショベル」,「スペシャル」,「バトル」のようなカタカナ発音にならないよう注意が必要である。

— …, teachers and faculty picking up rakes and *shovels*,…

(Columbine: 20 Years Later, p.84)

— …to the classroom, something *special*.

(America Strong: Foster Grandparents, p.9)

— *Battle* over funding for the *Special* Olympics.

(Special Olympics Funding Furor, p.54)

College Scandal Shock Waves

Air Date: March 12, 2019
Duration: 3' 13"

Preview Questions

1. What kind of scandal is taking place on American college campuses?

——アメリカの大学キャンパスではどのようなスキャンダルが起こっていますか。

2. How is it being dealt with?

——今はどのような状況ですか。

Warm-up Exercises

A Vocabulary Check: Choose the correct definition for each of the words below.

1. fallout ( )

2. sweeping ( )

3. scheme ( )

4. pose ( )

5. strive ( )

a. to make great efforts to achieve or obtain something

b. to pretend to be something

c. large-scale plan or strategy

d. negative consequences

e. extensive; wide-ranging

B Fill in the blanks with appropriate expressions from the Vocabulary Check above. Change the word form where necessary.

1. Dad always encourages us to (   ) to do our very best in school.

2. That chain of computer stores has a new (   ) to attract elderly customers.

3. If Prof. Brown becomes the new department chair, we can expect (   ) change in the curriculum.

4. The two thieves (   ) as cleaning staff to gain entry into the exclusive hotel.

5. If the (   ) from the scandal continues to grow, the president of the company may have to resign.

News Story [3′ 13″]

D. Muir: New fallout from that college admissions cheating scandal tonight.

Full House actress Lori Loughlin was arrested today and just a short time ago, appearing before a judge. We learned that *Desperate Housewives* actress Felicity Huffman was arrested in the last 24 hours by the FBI, their weapons drawn. And another arrest to report tonight, the USC's women's water polo head coach [1.] _____.

And tonight, this question: What about the children? The ones who authorities say did not know, and some who did, in fact, know what was happening. ABC's Kayna Whitworth at the federal courthouse tonight.

K. Whitworth: Tonight, Lori Loughlin set to be released on $1 million bond after being arrested today for her alleged role in that sweeping college bribery scheme.

L. Loughlin, actress (clip from TV show, Full House): You've worked very hard for your success. [2.] _____ _____, I know that I am.

K. Whitworth: The actress who played a
role model on *Full House* allegedly
shelling out $500,000 to consultant
Rick Singer, along with her fashion
designer husband, to get their
daughters into USC, posing them
as recruits for the crew team even
though they didn't row.

FBI agent: FBI! Warrant!

K. Whitworth: Arrest warrants issued for 46 people around the country,
3. _____

_____, like Felicity Huffman, seen here at the courthouse after
she was arrested by agents, guns drawn, and cuffed. Tonight, the actress
out of jail on $250,000 bond.

F. Huffman, actress (clip from TV show, Desperate Housewives): Are you
asking for a bribe?

Actor: Are you pretending you're above that?

F. Huffman: I'll get my checkbook.

K. Whitworth: The star of *Desperate Housewives* so desperate to land her
daughter in a top school, prosecutors say she paid $15,000 to Singer to
bribe a proctor who would secretly correct her answers. Prosecutors say
the scheme's mastermind **4.** _____

_____ to game the system.

A. Lelling, U.S. attorney, Massachusetts: For every student admitted through
fraud, an honest, genuinely talented student was rejected.

K. Whitworth: Today, on USC's campus, students told us they feel cheated.

H. Jain, USC graduate student: I feel for people like us who actually strive
hard day and night to just come here and learn.

K. Whitworth: The school firing legendary coach of the number one ranked
women's water polo team, **5.** _____

_____. He's facing charges for taking $250,000 in bribes. Also fired, senior associate athletic director Donna Heinel, accused of taking a whopping $1.3 million to push through fake athletic recruits, complete with photoshopped pictures.

D. Muir: So, let's get back to Kayna Whitworth on the story again tonight. She's live outside the federal courthouse in Los Angeles. And, Kayna, we know, prosecutors say that **6.** _____ _____, the students, were unaware, but it's believed some might have known. A lot of people are asking, what's gonna happen to some of these students?

K. Whitworth: Well, David, USC says they plan to conduct a case by case review of current students and graduates who may be involved with this scheme and **7.** _____ _____. UCLA adding that any student involved could face disciplinary action, including cancellation of admission. And, David, we have to keep in mind here that prosecutors are not ruling out additional charges.

Notes **college admissions cheating scandal**「大学（への）不正（裏口）入学スキャンダル（事件）」 **_Full House_**「『フルハウス』〈ABC 放送で 1987 年から 1995 年にかけて放送されたアメリカの大ヒットコメディドラマ。日本でも 1993 年から NHK 教育テレビで放送された〉」 **Lori Loughlin**「ロリ・ロックリン〈『フルハウス』でレベッカ役を演じて人気を博した〉」 **_Desperate Housewives_**「『デスパレートな妻たち』2004 年から 2012 年にかけて ABC 放送で放送されていた人気ドラマ〉」 **Felicity Huffman**「フェリシティ・ハフマン〈『デスパレートな妻たち』でリネット役を演じてエミー賞を受賞した〉」 **USC**＝巻末資料参照 **water polo**「水球」 **federal courthouse**「連邦裁判所」 **bond**「保釈金」 **alleged role ~**「〜に関与した疑いで」 **role model**「手本となる人物」 **allegedly ~**「〜したとされている」 **shelling out**「(大金を) 支払う」 **consultant Rick Singer**「(入試) コンサルタント (カウンセラー) のリック・シンガー〈進学カウンセリング会社を経営していた〉」 **recruits**「新人〈ボート経験がない娘 2 人をスポーツ枠で合格させるため，ボートを漕ぐ動きを練習する写真を撮影し，大学側に提出したという〉」 **Warrant!**「令状だ (逮捕する)！」 **Arrest warrants**「逮捕令状」 **Are you pretending you're above that?**「自分はそんなことするわけがないと言いたいのですか。〈Are you claiming that you are (morally/ethically) too good to do something like that?〉」 **land**「入学させる」 **proctor**「試験監督官」 **mastermind**「首謀者」 **game the system**「(入試) 制度の抜け穴を悪用 (巧妙に利用) する」 **U.S. attorney**「連邦検事」 **legendary coach**「伝説的コーチ」 **senior associate athletic director**「上級副体育局長〈ドナ・ハイネルは南カリフォルニア大学で体育会クラブを管理する役職に就いていた〉」 **whopping ~**「実に〜もの (大金)」 **push through ~**「無理やり〜を合格させる」 **complete with ~**「〜で仕上げる；加工する」 **photoshopped pictures**「フォトショップで加工 (偽造) された写真；画像処理ソフトで作られた合成 (偽造) 写真」 **disciplinary action**「懲戒処分」 **additional charges**「追加的な (さらなる) 告発」

Background of
the News

　2019年3月，南カリフォルニア大学（USC）やカリフォルニア大学ロサンゼルス校（UCLA）など一流大学への不正入学を請け負ったとして，連邦裁判所（federal courthouse）はブローカー役の進学カウンセリング会社経営の男を，組織的不正行為などの罪で起訴した。毎日新聞（2019/03/14）によると，首謀者（mastermind）のリック・シンガー（Rick Singer）は2011年以降，計761件の不正に携わり総額2,500万ドル（約27億8千万円）の賄賂（bribe）を受け取っていた。中には，中国人の富豪が娘のスタンフォード大学への入学のために，不正入学の賄賂としては最高額の650万ドル（約7億1千万円）を支払っていたケースもあったという。

　子供の裏口入学を依頼したとして訴追された保護者は33人で，弁護士や実業家のほか，アメリカ人気女優などのセレブが多く含まれていた。有名大学のスポーツ指導者9人も起訴された。他に裏口入学が行われたのは，ジョージタウン大学，エール大学などで，協力者がいる試験会場で替え玉受験を行ったり，試験監督官（proctor）を買収し，得点を水増しさせたりしていた。さらに，スポーツ推薦枠を悪用し，大学のコーチに賄賂を渡して競技経験のない受験生もスポーツ枠で不正に入学させていた。

After　You Watch the News

Exercises

A Listen to the CD and fill in the blanks in the text.　◎ CD 44

B Multiple Choice Questions

1. The parents involved in the cheating scandal did so
   a. because they could not afford to pay the tuition fees.
   b. to ensure that their children be admitted to top schools.
   c. to avoid having their children get kicked out of prestigious universities.

2. Consultant Rick Singer
   a. has been arrested and then released on bail.
   b. sometimes corrected exam answers for rich students.
   c. bribed others to get the children of wealthy parents into school.

3. Which of the following was part of the cheating scheme?

a. using photoshopped images to appeal to sports coaches

b. threatening college officials, with their weapons drawn

c. making sure that none of the children were aware of the cheating

4. According to the news story, what is most likely to happen?

a. Some famous actresses have been arrested and their children could face disciplinary action.

b. Some college officials have lost their jobs but the mastermind of the scheme might go free.

c. Some students could have their admission cancelled and other students who were rejected might get in.

C Translate the following Japanese into English. Then listen to the CD and practice the conversation with your partner. CD 45

A: Did you hear that Lori Loughlin was arrested today?

B: The actress from *Full House*? What did she do?

A: ¹_____

_____.

B: No way! Wait a minute—weren't those sisters on the USC crew team?

A: That's just it. ²_____

_____.

B: Fake athletes! Talented students were rejected and these students got in through fraud.

A: A lot of kids must be feeling really cheated. ³_____

_____.

1. 彼女と夫は，娘たちを USC に入学させるために巨額の賄賂を渡しました。

2. クルーチームの新人を装ったのですが，実際にはボートを漕いだことさえありませんでした。

3. もし，その学生たちが不正を知っていたのならば，みんな退学させられるべきです。

D Summary Practice: Fill in the blanks with suitable words beginning with the letters indicated.

⊙ CD 46

A sweeping scandal is playing out involving (¹· **c**   )
(²· **a**   ) in the U.S. Arrest (³· **w**   ) have
been issued for (⁴· **f**   )-(⁵· **s**   ) people alleged to have been involved
in the (⁶· **b**   ) (⁷· **s**   ), including famous
(⁸· **a**   ) Lori Loughlin and (⁹· **F**   )
(¹⁰· **H**   ). Loughlin and her (¹¹· **f**   ) designer
husband paid $(¹²· **f**   ) (¹³· **h**   ) (¹⁴· **t**   ) to
get their daughters into USC, relying on (¹⁵· **f**   ) athletic records and
(¹⁶· **p**   ) pictures. Huffman allegedly paid the
(¹⁷· **m**   ) of the operation, Rick Singer, to bribe a
(¹⁸· **p**   ) to (¹⁹· **c**   ) her daughter's test answers. The
(²⁰· **c**   ) of the number one ranked women's (²¹· **w**   )
(²²· **p**   ) team has been fired, along with an (²³· **a**   )
(²⁴· **d**   ) who accepted a (²⁵· **w**   ) $1.3 million
in bribes. The fate of the students themselves? That remains to be seen, but
USC plans to carry out a case by case (²⁶· **r**   ), and has not ruled
out (²⁷· **d**   ) action.

E Discussion: Share your ideas and opinions with your classmates.

1. News of the college admissions cheating scandal came as a great shock to many people in the U.S. Have there been any admissions scandals at Japanese universities in recent years?

2. A number of prominent celebrities and sports directors were found to be involved in this scandal. Why do you think they would do such a thing? What do you think would be fair punishment for them?

3. As a college student, how do you think the students involved in these cases should be treated? Are they also guilty, or are they victims? How would you feel if you learned that someone pulled some strings to get you into the university of your choice? Discuss your answers with your classmates.

Appendix
巻末資料

Map of the United States 96

TVニュース英語とは 98

最近のTVニュースに現れた略語 104

Map of the Un

CANADA

❼
Washington

Montana

North Dakota

Minneso

Oregon

Idaho

South Dakota

Wyoming

❻

Nevada

Nebraska

Io

❽

Utah

❿
Colorado

❹

California

Kansas

❸

❺

Arizona

New Mexico

Oklahoma

Alaska

Texas

MEXICO

Hawaii

ed States

❶〜⓫はニュースに登場し
た都市名で，州名はイタリ
ックになっています。
各都市の位置は，地図上に
番号で示しています。

News Story 1
Tennessee
❶Washington, D.C.

News Story 2
❶Washington, D.C.

News Story 3
❷Parkland, *Florida*
❸Las Vegas, *Nevada*

News Story 5   *Alabama*

News Story 6   *California*

News Story 8   *Florida*
                     Kentucky

News Story 9
❹Santa Cruz

News Story 10
❶Washington, D.C.

News Story 11   *Florida*

News Story 12
❺Los Angeles, *California*

News Story 13
❻Oakland, *California*
❼Seattle, Washington
❽San Jose, *California*
❾Chicago, *Illinois*

News Story 14
❿Columbine, *Colorado*
Virginia
⓫Sandy Hook, *Connecticut*
❷Parkland, *Florida*
Florida

News Story 15
Hawaii
❺Los Angeles, *California*

TVニュース英語とは

1 アメリカ国内テレビニュース英語の特徴

　本書は直接ニューヨークで受信したテレビニュースから素材を選定し，米国 ABC 放送局本社からニュース映像を提供してもらいテキストに編集している。

　ニュース英語は伝えるメディア媒体の種類上，大きく分けて３種類に分類される。第１は新聞，雑誌などに代表される活字で伝えられるもの，第２にはラジオのように音声情報に頼る媒体から提供されるもの，そして第３番目はネットやテレビを介して音声情報と画像情報が同時に供給されるニュースである。ここでは，第３番目のメディア媒体であるテレビ放送におけるニュース英語の特徴を簡単にまとめてみた。ニュース英語というと使用される英語もフォーマルなイメージがあるが，実際には以下で述べるように口語的な特徴も多く見られる。ここで引用している例文は最近の *ABC World News Tonight* で実際使われたものばかりである。

1.1 ニュースの構成

　まず，放送スタジオにいるアンカーパーソンが，そのニュースの中心情報をリード部分で述べ，何についてのニュースであるかを視聴者に知らせる。アンカーパーソンは，ごく短くそのニュースの概要を紹介し，リポーターへとバトンタッチする。次にリポーターが現地からのリポートを，時にはインタビュー等を交えながら詳しく報告する，というのがテレビニュースの一般的なパターンになっている。それを略図で示したのが次の図である。ひとつのニュースの放送時間は割合短く，普通 1.5 〜 3 分程である。

●ニュースの構成

Anchor, Anchorperson

LEAD
INTRODUCTION（放送スタジオ）

リポーターへの導入表現

Reporter

MAIN BODY（現地からのリポート，
　　　　　　　　インタビューなど）

リポーターの結びの表現

1.2 比較的速いスピード

発話速度はセンター入試のリスニング問題で平均毎分約 155 ～ 160 語，英検 2 級では 150 語前後ぐらいだと言われている。しかし，生の（authentic）英語になると，かなり発話速度が速くなる。英語母語話者が話す速度は，インフォーマルな会話の場合，平均毎分 210 語で，速い場合は人によって 230 wpm (words per minute) になる。典型的なフォーマル・スタイルの英語である，アメリカ国内のテレビニュース放送（ABC 放送）を筆者が調べたところ，発話速度は平均 163 ～ 198 wpm であることが分かった。生の英語でも一般的にフォーマルな話しことばほど発話速度は落ちてくるが，アメリカ国内用のテレビニュースは比較的速い方に分類される。

1.3 不完全文の多用

テレビニュース英語では，be 動詞や主語，動詞が省略された「不完全文」が多く，端的で箇条書き的な表現が好んで使われる。例えば，以下の例は ABC 放送で実際に使用されていた文である。これらは散列文（loose sentence）として，書きことばでは非文とされるが，テレビニュース英語ではよく現れる不完全文の一例と考えられる。

— Tonight, fears the U.S. is on the brink of an outbreak among the birds.

上記を補足的に書き換えると以下のようになる。

— Tonight, [there are] fears [that] the U.S. is on the brink of an outbreak [of bird flu] among the birds.

次は，シェイクスピアが人気があることを伝えるニュースからの例である。

— Four hundred years, 20 generations and still going strong.

これを，説明的に補足すれば，以下のようになる。

— Four hundred years [or] 20 generations [have passed since he died and he is] still going strong.

新聞英語の見出しでは be 動詞が省略されることはよく知られているが，テレビニュース英語では，主語・一般動詞・be 動詞・関係代名詞などを省略し，箇条書き的な文体で情報を生き生きと伝える。文法より，伝達する意味内容を重視するため，短い語句をたたみかけるように次々つなぐのである。特に，ニュースの冒頭部分で何についての報道であるか，そのトピックを告げるときにこの文体はよく用いられる。以下の（∧）は，そこに何らかの項目が省略されていることを示している。

— ∧ Sixty-nine years old, ∧ married for 35 years, ∧ lives in Honolulu.
— The weather was calm, the tide ∧ high, ...
— This is the fifth anniversary of the Columbine tragedy, ∧ the worst school shooting in U.S. history.
— Today, ∧ the battle for Ohio.

このような不完全文を使うことによって，ニュースに緊張感や臨場感を持たせ，視聴者の興味を引き付けている。テレビニュースの場合は視聴者の視覚に訴える画像情報があるので，完全で説明的な文体を使用するよりは，むしろ箇条書的な不完全文の方が視聴者にアピールしやすい。

1.4 現在時制が多い

最新のニュースを伝えるというテレビニュースの即時性を考えれば，現在形や近い未来を表す表現が多いことは容易に予想される。米 ABC 放送のニュースにおける時制について調べたところ，現在形と現在進行形で 46% を占めていることが分かった。現在形や進行形の多用は臨場感を生み出す。

— The world's largest carmakers say they **are going to** lower the frame on sport utility vehicles...
— ..., and Rome's police **are** aggressively **enforcing** the new law, ...
— Americans now **spend** more time on the job than workers in any other developed country.
— ...their budget shortfalls **are** so severe they **are going** to raise taxes.
— Now AmeriCorps **is telling** future volunteers there may be no place for them.

新聞などの書きことばにおけるニュース英語では, 未来を表すのに "be expected to", "be scheduled to", "be to" などやや固い表現がよく使われるが，口語的なニュース英語では "will" が好んで使用される。

— In this crowd, there are damning claims that she is being starved, that she **will** suffer.
— For now, some colleges **will** ignore scores for the new writing section, ...

1.5 伝達動詞は say が多い

ニュース英語の特徴として「誰々がこう言った，何々によればこういうことである」といった構文が多く現れる。主語＋伝達動詞＋（that）節という構文では，伝達動詞は say が圧倒的に多く用いられる。構文に変化を付けるために，主節が文中に挿入されたり、文尾に後置されたりする場合も多い。

— One result of higher temperatures, **says** the government, is more extremes in the weather, ...
— But that's the male reaction, **say** the researchers.

直接話法では，Mary said to Cathy, "I like your new car." というように，「発言者＋伝達動詞」が被伝達部に先行するのが一般的である。ニュースの英語では，このような直接話法を使って「…が〜と言いました」という表現はよく見られるが，以下のように「発言者＋伝達動詞」が被伝達部の後に出てくる場合も多い。また，以下の冒頭例のように，発言

者が人称代名詞以外の名詞であれば，伝達動詞が先に来る。

— "It turns out they're a lot more like people than we thought," **says** the director of the Wolong reserve.
— "I'm going to use an expression," he **says**.
— "It's strange to be here," he **says**.
— "Soon, we're planning to fly from Baghdad to Europe," he **says**.

1.6 縮約形の多用

　以下のような指示代名詞，人称代名詞や疑問代名詞の後の be 動詞，助動詞の縮約形（contraction）がよく使われる：it's, that's, we'll, don't, I'm, you're, here's, they're, we're, we've, can't, won't, what's.

　縮約形はくだけた会話英語の特徴である。以下の例からも分かるように，テレビニュース英語では新聞英語とは異なって，縮約形の使用によりインフォーマルな雰囲気が出ている。書きことばの原稿をただ読み上げるのではなくて，視聴者にとって親しみやすい響きを与える口語的なスタイルが心がけられている。

— And the reason why, George, is **they've** learned that the Made in the USA tag carries real weight in China.
— **It's** been decades since then, but polio is still very much alive.
— Add it all up and America's happiest person **isn't** Tom Selleck, **it's** Alvin Wong.
— ..., the one that comes when you **can't** put down the Blackberry or iPhone at home, ...
— **She's** constantly juggling his needs and those of the Cincinnati ad agency she works for.

2 テレビニュースの表現

2.1 冒頭部分の特徴

　ストーリーの全体を予想させたり，ニュース内容に期待を持たせたりするために，ニュースの冒頭には短いインパクトのある表現や，やや大げさな表現が置かれる。以下の例は気球に乗って初めて世界一周に成功した人のニュースである。

— **History was made today** above the Sahara Desert — man, for the first time, has flown around the world nonstop in a balloon.

　新聞英語では，冒頭の文（lead）で読者の注意をひきつけるために，書き方が工夫されることが多い。テレビニュース英語でも，新しいニュースの始まりの部分では疑問文，繰り返し，文法的に不完全な文などを用いて視聴者の興味をひきつけようとする。

— Finally this evening, *not just another pretty face*.

— *The weather, the weather, always the weather.*

— Finally, this evening, *will they turn the panda cam back on again?*

2.2 リポーター紹介の表現

　アンカーパーソンがニュースの主要情報を紹介した後，リポーターにバトンタッチする時の表現である。日本語のニュースでは「では，現場の〜がリポートします」に当たる部分で，次のように様々なバリエーションがある。

— And tonight, Dr. Richard Besser takes us to a remote part of the world, ...

— ABC's Abbie Boudreau is in Provo, Utah.

— It's a duel in the Capitol Hill cafeteria and Jon Karl explains.

— We asked Bianna Golodryga to find out.

— Lisa Stark explains why.

— Here's John Berman on health, wealth and birth order.

— Jim Avila is at a McDonald's in Newark, New Jersey, tonight. Jim?

　アンカーパーソンが，現場のリポーターや別の放送スタジオにいるニュースキャスターを呼び出す時には，その人にファーストネームで呼びかける。呼びかけられた人は，自分の読む原稿が終了して元のアンカーパーソンに戻したい時にもまたファーストネームで呼びかける。名前の呼び合いがバトンタッチの合図にもなっている。

— **D. Sawyer:** Jim Avila is at a McDonald's in Newark, New Jersey, tonight. *Jim?*

— **J. Avila:** Well, *Diane*, in this one McDonald's alone, more than 1,000 people applied for what's likely to be four jobs.

— **J. Karl:** ..., it's probably going to last in a landfill somewhere for thousands and thousands of years. *Diane?*

— **D. Sawyer:** Okay, *Jon*. That was one sad spoon earlier.

2.3 リポーターの結びの表現

　リポーターは現場からの報道の最後を決まりきった表現で結ぶ。リポーターの名前，放送局，リポート地が告げられる。それぞれの間にポーズを入れ，すこしゆっくり目に言われるのが共通した特徴である。

— John Berman, ABC News, New York.

— Lisa Stark, ABC News, Washington.

— Barbara Pinto, ABC News, Chicago.

— Jeffrey Kofman, ABC News, Nairobi.

2.4 ニュースとニュースのつなぎ表現

ひとつのニュースから別のニュースに移行する時，何らかのシグナルがある方が視聴者としても分かりやすい。後続のニュース内容に応じた様々な表現を使って新しいニュースの始まりを合図している。

— ***And finally tonight,*** what makes someone the happiest person in America?
— ***Now to a story about*** the struggle between technology and family time.
— ***And finally,*** our "Person of the Week."
— ***And now, we move on to*** an incredible scene across the country today beneath the iconic symbol of corporate America, McDonald's.
— ***Tonight,*** we want to tell you about something new in the use of brain surgery to control tremors from a number of causes.

2.5 コマーシャル前のつなぎの表現

コマーシャルの間にチャンネルを変えられないよう，次のニュースの予告をする際，以下のような様々な工夫した表現が使われる。

— And when we come back, a master class in enduring crisis from the Japanese people.
— And coming up next, what's become one of those annual rites of spring.
— When we come back here on the broadcast tonight, we switch gears and take a look at this.

2.6 番組終了時の表現

その日のニュース番組は，挨拶や次回の予告などで終わる。

— And be sure to watch "Nightline" later on tonight. Our co-anchor Bill Weir is here — right here in Japan, as well.
— And we'll see you back here from Japan tomorrow night. Until then we hope you have a good night at home in the United States.
— And that's it from us for now.

最近のニュースに現れた略語

▼A

AAA [Automobile Association of America] 全米自動車連盟

AARP [American Association of Retired Persons] 全米退職者協会

ABA [American Bar Association] 米国弁護士協会

ABC [American Broadcasting Companies] ABC放送

ABC [American-born Chinese] アメリカ生まれの中国人

ACA [Affordable Care Act] 医療費負担適正化法

ACLU [American Civil Liberties Union] 米国自由人権協会

ACT [American College Test] 米大学入学学力テスト

ADHD [attention-deficit hyperactivity disorder] 注意欠陥・多動性障害

AI [artificial intelligence] 人工知能

AIDS [acquired immune deficiency syndrome] 後天性免疫不全症候群

AMA [American Medical Association] 米国医師会

ANC [African National Congress] アフリカ民族会議

AOL [America Online] アメリカ・オンライン：アメリカのパソコン通信大手

AP [Associated Press] AP通信社：アメリカ最大の通信社

ASEAN [Association of Southeast Asian Nations] アセアン；東南アジア諸国連合

ATF [Federal Bureau of Alcohol, Tobacco and Firearms] アルコール・たばこ・火器局 [米]

ATM [automated teller (telling) machine] 現金自動預け払い機

AT&T [American Telephone and Telegraph Corporation] 米国電話電信会社

ATV [all-terrain vehicle] オフロードカー

▼B

BART [Bay Area Rapid Transit] バート：サンフランシスコ市の通勤用高速鉄道

BBC [British Broadcasting Corporation] 英国放送協会

BYU [Brigham Young University] ブリガム・ヤング大学

▼C

CBO [Congressional Budget Office] 連邦議会予算局

CBS [Columbia Broadcasting System] （米国）コロンビア放送会社

CCTV [China Central Television] 国営中国中央テレビ

CDC [Centers for Disease Control and Prevention] 疾病対策センター [米]

CEO [chief executive officer] 最高経営役員

CHP [Department of California Highway Patrol] カリフォルニア・ハイウェイ・パトロール

CIA [Central Intelligence Agency] 中央情報局 [米]

CNN [Cable News Network] シー・エヌ・エヌ

COLA [cost-of-living adjustment] 生活費調整

COO [chief operating officer] 最高執行責任者

CPSC [(U.S.) Consumer Product Safety Commission] 米消費者製品安全委員会

CT [computerized tomography] CTスキャン；コンピュータ断層撮影

▼D

DC [District of Columbia] コロンビア特別区

DHS [Department of Homeland Security] 国土安全保障省［米］

DJIA [Dow Jones Industrial Average] ダウ（ジョーンズ）工業株30種平均

DMV [Department of Motor Vehicles] 自動車局：車両登録や運転免許を扱う

DMZ [Demilitarized Zone] 非武装地帯

DNA [deoxyribonucleic acid] デオキシリボ核酸：遺伝子の本体

DNC [Democratic National Committee] 民主党全国委員会

DOD [Department of Defense] アメリカ国防総省

DPRK [Democratic People's Republic of Korea] 朝鮮民主主義人民共和国

DST [Daylight Saving Time] サマータイム；夏時間

DVD [digital versatile disc] ディーブイディー：大容量光ディスクの規格

DWI [driving while intoxicated] 酒酔い運転；酒気帯び運転

▼E

EDT [Eastern Daylight (saving) Time] 東部夏時間［米］

EMS [European Monetary System] 欧州通貨制度

EPA [Environmental Protection Agency] 環境保護庁［米］

ER [emergency room] 救急処置室

ES cell [embryonic stem cell] ES細胞；胚性幹細胞：あらゆる種類の組織・臓器に分化できる細胞

EU [European Union] 欧州連合

EV [electric(al) vehicle] 電気自動車

▼F

FAA [Federal Aviation Administration] 連邦航空局［米］

FBI [Federal Bureau of Investigation] 連邦捜査局［米］

FCC [Federal Communications Commission] 連邦通信委員会［米］

FDA [Food and Drug Administration] 食品医薬品局［米］

FEMA [Federal Emergency Management Agency] 連邦緊急事態管理局［米］

FIFA [Federation of International Football Associations (Fédération Internationale de Football Association)] フィーファ；国際サッカー連盟

FRB [Federal Reserve Bank] 連邦準備銀行［米］

FRB [Federal Reserve Board] 連邦準備制度理事会［米］

FTC [Federal Trade Commission] 連邦取引委員会［米］

FWS [Fish and Wildlife Service] 魚類野生生物局［米］

▼G

G8 [the Group of Eight] 先進（主要）８カ国（首脳会議）

G-20 [the Group of Twenty (Finance Ministers and Central Bank Governors)] 主要20カ国・地域財務相・中央銀行総裁会議

GAO [General Accounting Office] 会計検査院［米］

GDP [gross domestic product] 国内総生産

GE [General Electric Company] ゼネラル・エレクトリック：アメリカの大手総合電機メーカー

GM [General Motors Corporation] ゼネラル・モーターズ社：アメリカの大手自動車メーカー

GMA [Good Morning America] グッド・モーニング・アメリカ〈ABC放送の朝の情報・ニュース番組〉

GMT [Greenwich Mean Time] グリニッジ標準時

GNP [gross national product] 国民総生産

GOP [Grand Old Party] ゴップ：アメリカ共和党の異名

GPA [grade point average] 成績平均点

GPS [global positioning system] 全地球測位システム

▼H

HBO [Home Box Office] ホーム・ボックス・オフィス：アメリカ最大手のペイケーブル番組供給業者

HHS [Department of Health and Human Services] 保健社会福祉省［米］

HIV [human immunodeficiency virus] ヒト免疫不全ウイルス

HMO [Health Maintenance Organization] 保健維持機構［米］

HMS [Her (His) Majesty's Ship] 英国海軍；英国海軍艦船

HRW [Human Rights Watch] ヒューマン・ライツ・ウォッチ

HSBC [Hongkong and Shanghai Banking Corporation Limited] 香港上海銀行

▼I

IBM [International Business Machines Corporation] アイ・ビー・エム

ICBM [intercontinental ballistic missile] 大陸間弾道ミサイル（弾）

ICE [Immigration and Customs Enforcement] 移民税関捜査局［米］

ID [identification] 身分証明書

IDF [Israel Defense Forces] イスラエル国防軍

IMF [International Monetary Fund] 国際通貨基金

Inc. [~ Incorporated] ～会社；会社組織の；有限会社

INS [Immigration and Naturalization Service] 米国移民帰化局

IOC [International Olympic Committee] 国際オリンピック委員会

IPCC [Intergovernmental Panel on Climate Change] 気候変動に関する政府間パネル

IQ [intelligence quotient] 知能指数

IRA [Irish Republican Army] アイルランド共和軍

IRS	[Internal Revenue Service] 内国歳入庁［米］
ISIS	[Islamic State of Iraq and Syria] イスラム国
IT	[information technology] 情報テクノロジー；情報技術
IUCN	[International Union for Conservation of Nature (and Natural Resources)] 国際自然保護連合

▼J

JCAHO	[Joint Commission on Accreditation of Healthcare Organizations] 医療施設認定合同審査会［米］
JFK	[John Fitzgerald Kennedy] ケネディー：アメリカ第35代大統領

▼L

LA	[Los Angeles] ロサンゼルス
LED	[light-emitting diode] 発光ダイオード
LLC	[limited liability company] 有限責任会社
LNG	[liquefied natural gas] 液化天然ガス

▼M

M&A	[merger and acquisition] 企業の合併・買収
MADD	[Mothers Against Drunk Driving] 酒酔い運転に反対する母親の会［米］
MERS	[Middle East Respiratory Syndrome (coronavirus)] マーズコロナウイルス
MLB	[Major League Baseball] メジャー・リーグ・ベースボール［米］
MMR	[measles-mumps-rubella vaccine] MMRワクチン：はしか，おたふく風邪，風疹の３種混合の予防接種
MRI	[magnetic resonance imaging] 磁気共鳴映像法
MVP	[most valuable player] 最高殊勲選手；最優秀選手

▼N

NAFTA	[North Atlantic Free Trade Area] ナフタ；北大西洋自由貿易地域
NASA	[National Aeronautics and Space Administration] 航空宇宙局［米］
NASCAR	[National Association for Stock Car Auto Racing] 全米自動車競争協会
NASDAQ	[National Association of Securities Dealers Automated Quotations]（証券）ナスダックシステム；相場情報システム［米］
NATO	[North Atlantic Treaty Organization] 北大西洋条約機構
NBA	[National Basketball Association] 全米バスケットボール協会
NBC	[National Broadcasting Company] NBC放送
NCAA	[National Collegiate Athletic Association] 全米大学体育協会
NCIC	[National Crime Information Center] 全米犯罪情報センター
NFL	[National Football League] ナショナル［米プロ］・フットボール・リーグ
NGO	[non-governmental organization] 非政府（間）組織；民間非営利団体
NHL	[National Hockey League] 北米プロアイスホッケー・リーグ

NHTSA [National Highway Traffic Safety Administration] 幹線道路交通安全局［米］
NIH [National Institutes of Health] 国立保健研究［米］
NRA [National Rifle Association] 全米ライフル協会
NSA [National Security Agency] 国家安全保障局［米］
NTSA [National Technical Services Association] 全国輸送安全委員会［米］
NTSB [National Transportation Safety Board] 国家運輸安全委員会［米］
NV [Nevada] ネバダ州（アメリカ）
NYPD [New York City Police Department] ニューヨーク市警察

▼O
OMB [the Office of Management and Budget] 行政管理予算局
OPEC [Organization of Petroleum Exporting Countries] 石油輸出国機構

▼P
PGA [Professional Golfers' Association] プロゴルフ協会〈正式には，全米プロゴルフ協会はProfessional Golfers' Association of America（PGA of America）〉
PGD [pre-implantation genetic diagnosis] 着床前遺伝子診断
PIN [personal identification number] 暗証番号；個人識別番号
PLO [Palestine Liberation Organization] パレスチナ解放機構
POW [prisoner of war] 戦争捕虜
PVC [polyvinyl chloride] ポリ塩化ビニル

▼Q
QB [quarterback] クォーターバック（アメリカン・フットボール）

▼R
RAF [Royal Air Force] 英国空軍
RNC [Republican National Committee] 共和党全国委員会
ROK [Republic of Korea] 大韓民国
ROTC [Reserve Officers' Training Corps] 予備役将校訓練団［米］
RV [recreational vehicle] リクリエーション用自動車

▼S
SAM [surface-to-air missile] 地対空ミサイル
SARS [Severe Acute Respiratory Syndrome] 重症急性呼吸器症候群
SAT [Scholastic Aptitude Test] 大学進学適性試験［米］
SEC [(U.S.) Securities and Exchange Commission] 米証券取引委員会
SNS [social networking service] ソーシャル・ネットワーキング・サービス：インターネットを介して，友人や知人の輪を広げていくためのオンラインサービス
START [Strategic Arms Reduction Treaty] 戦略兵器削減条約
STD [sexually transmitted (transmissible) diseases] 性感染症

SUV [sport-utility vehicle] スポーツ・ユーティリティ・ビークル；スポーツ汎用車

SWAT [Special Weapons and Tactics] スワット；特別機動隊［米］

▼T

TB [tuberculosis] 結核

TOB [takeover bid] 株式の公開買付制度：企業の支配権を得るためにその企業の株式を買い集めること

TPP [Trans-Pacific Partnership] 環太平洋戦略的経済連携協定

TSA [Transportation Security Administration] 運輸保安局［米］

▼U

UA [United Airlines] ユナイテッド航空

UAE [United Arab Emirates] アラブ首長国連邦

UAW [United Automobile Workers] 全米自動車労働組合

UCLA [University of California at Los Angeles] カリフォルニア大学ロサンゼルス校

UK [United Kingdom (of Great Britain and Northern Ireland)] 英国；グレートブリテンおよび北部アイルランド連合王国：英国の正式名

UN [United Nations] 国際連合

UNICEF [United Nations International Children's Emergency Fund] ユニセフ；国連児童基金〈現在の名称はUnited Nations Children's Fund〉

USAF [United States Air Force] 米空軍

USC [the University of Southern California] 南カリフォルニア大学

USDA [United States Department of Agriculture] 米農務省

USGS [United States Geological Survey] 米国地質調査所

USMC [United States Marine Corps] 米国海兵隊

このテキストのメインページ
www.kinsei-do.co.jp/plusmedia/40

次のページの QR コードを読み取る
直接ページにジャンプできます

オンライン映像配信サービス「plus⁺Media」について

本テキストの映像は plus⁺Media ページ（www.kinsei-do.co.jp/plusmedia）から、ストリーミング再生でご利用いただけます。手順は以下に従ってください。

ログイン

ログインページ

● ご利用には、ログインが必要です。
サイトのログインページ（www.kinsei-do.co.jp/plusmedia/login）へ行き、plus⁺Media パスワード（次のページのシールをはがしたあとに印字されている数字とアルファベット）を入力します。

● パスワードは各テキストにつき 1 つです。
有効期限は、<u>はじめてログインした時点から 1 年間</u>になります。

[利用方法]

次のページにある QR コード、もしくは plus⁺Media トップページ（www.kinsei-do.co.jp/plusmedia）から該当するテキストを選んで、そのテキストのメインページにジャンプしてください。

メニューページ　　　　　再生画面

plus+Media トップ　　　メインページ

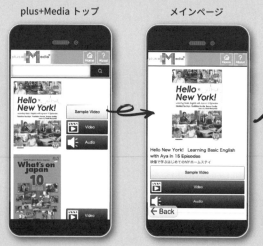

「Video」「Audio」をタッチすると、それぞれのメニューページにジャンプしますので、そこから該当する項目を選べば、ストリーミングが開始されます。

[推奨環境]

iOS (iPhone, iPad)	OS: iOS 6 〜 13　ブラウザ: 標準ブラウザ	Android	OS: Android 4.x 〜 9.0　ブラウザ: 標準ブラウザ、Chrome
PC	OS: Windows 7/8/8.1/10, MacOS X　ブラウザ: Internet Explorer 10/11, Microsoft Edge, Firefox 48以降, Chrome 53以降, Safari		

※ 最新の推奨環境についてはウェブサイトをご確認ください。

※ 上記の推奨環境を満たしている場合でも、機種によってはご利用いただけない場合もあります。また、推奨環境は技術動向等により変更される場合があります。予めご了承ください。

このシールをはがすと
plus+Media 利用のための
パスワードが
記載されています。

一度はがすと元に戻すことは
できませんのでご注意下さい。

◀ ここからはがして下さい

4096 Broadcast: ABC
WORLD NEWS TONIGHT 2

plus+Media

本書には CD（別売）があります

Broadcast: ABC WORLD NEWS TONIGHT 2

映像で学ぶ ABCワールドニュース 2

2020年1月20日　初版第1刷発行
2020年2月20日　初版第2刷発行

編著者　　山 根　　繁
　　　　　Kathleen Yamane

発行者　　福 岡 正 人
発行所　　株式会社　金 星 堂

（〒101-0051）東京都千代田区神田神保町 3-21
Tel. (03) 3263-3828（営業部）
(03) 3263-3997（編集部）
Fax (03) 3263-0716
http://www.kinsei-do.co.jp

編集担当　松本明子　　　　　　　　　Printed in Japan
印刷所・製本所／大日本印刷株式会社

ISBN978-4-7647-4096-9 C1082